Jacob

Extraordinary Character Collection: Volume One

A Novel

Based on the Award Winning Screenplay

-By-

Brett Scott Ermilio

Copyright 2014 by B.S. Ermilio Ltd.
All rights reserved. Published in the United States.
This is a work of fiction. Names, characters, places and incidents either are the product of the author's imagination or are used fictitiously. Any resemblance to actual persons, living or dead, events, or locales is entirely coincidental.
ISBN: 978-0-9863512-1-1
Edited by Laura Duane
Cover Design by Justin Brock
Formatting by Taylor J. Tims

For My Mother,
Jacob's Biggest Fan

Acknowledgments

I am thankful for the following people and their support:

First and foremost, my love, my wife. She enables everything that I am.

To my children, Phoenix, Bailey, Tyler and Ella—you are my little dreamers.

To my mother who has loved Jacob since he was born.

To my sister, Shere, and her undying support.

To my best friend in the world, and brother at arms, Robert Tyler Schwartz.

Thank you for always being there.

To Robert Entous who always believed in the spirit of Jacob.

To Laura Duane who makes me look good.

To Brielle Benton who gave me ample support in bringing Jacob to life.

To Taylor J. Tims who gave me great advice and brought it all together.

And finally, to Jacob, a dreamer who inspires me every single day.

Table of Contents

PROLOGUE	1
CHAPTER 1	2
CHAPTER 2	6
CHAPTER 3	11
CHAPTER 4	19
CHAPTER 5	30
CHAPTER 6	43
CHAPTER 7	50
CHAPTER 8	59
CHAPTER 9	62
CHAPTER 10	71
CHAPTER 11	83
CHAPTER 12	95
CHAPTER 13	100
CHAPTER 14	104
CHAPTER 15	114
CHAPTER 16	131
CHAPTER17	140
CHAPTER18	154
CHAPTER 19	174
CHAPTER 20	189
CHAPTER 21	201
CHAPTER 22	207
CHAPTER 23	213
CHAPTER 24	219
CHAPTER 25	222

Prologue

This is a story of a boy who changed the lives of everyone he came in contact with. He never grew up to be a great man whose name adorned stadium walls or parks. He didn't cure any diseases or climb Mount Everest. His name won't be repeated in any history books. His life began inside the confines of a small town: Starktown, Illinois. Not impressive in size, Starktown gave birth to one of the world's greatest dreamers ever known. His name was Jacob.

One

Towering green giants stand a hundred feet tall in all directions. Their thick, dark red, massive bodies harvest the souls of giants who have lived for centuries. Their arms reach out far and wide in all directions, providing an umbrella of safety from the dark skies above. Their fingers are brittle, and sharp, warmly touching their neighbors like old close friends.

The moon tries to penetrate the great oaks, but fails miserably. Standing among the mighty oaks in the pale of the moonlight is a figure. His gentle gray eyes catch momentary glimpses of the moon above. His face is as gentle as his eyes; unblemished, with perfect creamy white skin, as soft and smooth as a baby's bottom. His body is frail, although he stands almost six feet tall. He looks like a boy, but behind his sea of gray resides a man. He walks as if in some kind of trance, his steps slow and true, gliding across the ground.

A cold breeze dances through his fine dirty blond hair. He's not cold, despite his warm breaths visible in the chilly air. His white flannel pajamas protect him from the cold, while his curiosity distracts him just enough to stay away from any icy thoughts.

"*Arhee-arhee-arhee!*" echoes through the forest. It's a sharp loud cackle made by an insane animal.

The boy turns, glancing around in all directions, the cackle bringing him out of his trance. A rush of fear overwhelms him. Thoughts race through his mind, none of them making any sense. He's standing in the center of the forest. He looks down and sees his pajamas on. He's barefoot and now realizes he's cold.

"Jacob," whispers a voice in the forest.

The boy turns to find the voice, but finds only darkness. "Jacob," he hears again.

The boy whips his head around in all directions, unable to see anything but darkness. The cold, the noises, and the night seem to be attacking the boy all at once. He is becoming overwhelmed.

"JACOB!"

The boy takes off and runs. He's frightened and dashes as fast as he can. He runs for his life, afraid of what lurks behind him in the darkness. He glances back repeatedly, seeing nothing. But he knows something's there; he feels it.

The sky above grumbles, growling with anger. Thunder rolls and a stroke of lightning shoots down from the sky. It comes dangerously close to hitting the giants above him.

The boy looks up as teardrops fall from the sky. They fall slow at first, then the sky opens up, releasing all of its pain. Rain pours down on him.

The boy immediately becomes drenched. His fine flowing hair is sopping wet, hanging down in front of his eyes. He has trouble seeing and wipes his drenched hair away from his face.

Thunder rolls in the sky above.

Lightning shoots down from the sky and strikes a mighty oak, setting it ablaze.

Sparks from the flaming tree spray down upon the boy, joining the pouring rain. The oak starts to rupture, cracking in half, a large branch falling to the ground below. The boy runs away, narrowly avoiding the burning tree limb.

The thunder roars once again. But this time, the rumble is angry and is intended for the boy.

The boy places his hands over his ears, the roar becoming unbearable. Each stride is taken in a puddle of water but his white pajamas remain untarnished.

A lightning bolt shoots down from the sky and strikes the ground just in front of the boy. The boy falls to the ground, covering his eyes, the light blinding him.

His eyes flash open in horror. The scene has changed. Now the boy is submerged in water, sitting at the bottom of a lake. He tries to swim up but cannot. A metal shackle is latched around his ankle. The shackle in anchored to a giant metal ball resting comfortably at the bottom of the lake. The boy struggles with all his might to break free of the shackle, but it's to no avail. The fight begins to leave his body as he slowly floats down, further away from the light at the surface of the water, accepting death. Listless in the water, the boy senses something. Using his last bit of strength, he turns. Once turned, his eyes flare open in horror. His arms rise up just as a massive great white shark opens its jaws, showcasing layers and layers of sharpened bloody teeth. The shark's mouth is about to consume him when—

    Jacob sits up in a pool of sweat. He's breathing heavily and still reeling from his sequence of nightmares. He looks over his white pajamas, making sure his body is all in one piece. He wipes his dampened hair away from his face and cleans off any remnant of forehead sweat with his pajama sleeve. Jacob is a frail sixteen year old boy, a slightly older version of the young boy from his nightmare. He is oddly similar to the boy in his dream, physically almost identical to the dirty-blond haired boy. He lacks facial hair of any kind, feeding his fresh youthful appearance. A deep breath taken is an attempt to alleviate some of Jacob's nerves.

    The young man is wound up from his exhilarating adventure but shows no signs of being scared. He rubs his hands over his face and lets out a ferocious yawn. Content with himself and his surroundings, Jacob shuffles out of bed and moves across his pitch-black room. He powers on his computer and sits down before it.

    Jacob stays there, sitting in front of the bright white screen. The light from the computer shines upon his face the brightness of the light compounded by the dark abyss surrounding him. Jacob looks like an angel.

Two poker hands appear on the computer screen. Jacob sits by himself playing in the dark of night. He plays deep into early morning's darkness, all alone.

Two

The air is chilly and dew coats everything. A thick layer of fog has made the world completely gray, including the peeled off-white paint of the quaint two-story colonial. Surrounded by two mighty oaks on either side, the Crestwood home stands well-spaced from a flourish of other homes just down the street. The Crestwood home is the bridge between the lush green hills marking the lands of Mother Nature's belly and the small quaint suburban confines of Starktown, Illinois.

Many early black-faced, red-bodied cardinals hop around, pecking at the soil searching for stray night crawlers. It is a casually serene morning until…

Music bursts out from the Crestwood household; precisely, Jacob's bedroom. It's Randy Newman's energetic ballad, "I Love LA."

Ryan Crestwood's head pops up out of his off-white down comforter, his eyes flaring open, brought abruptly out of his deep sleep. Ryan's wavy dark hair hangs half in front of his well-tanned skin. He has the eyes of a tired old soul even though he's only lived twenty-six years on this earth. He shares the same soft skin as his younger brother, but carries responsibility inside his blue eyes and a wealth of frustration to go along with it.

"Jacob," mumbles an annoyed and tired Ryan, not the first time he's been awakened in this fashion by his younger brother.

He lets out a breath of swelling frustration, well aware of who's responsible for the early morning concert. The music penetrates Ryan's ears like an annoying bug flying about his face. He takes another deep breath and rolls his tired body out of bed, tossing aside his comforter.

Bouncing up and down in fuzzy ducky slippers and oversized freakish orange sun-glasses is an exuberant Jacob.

He's possessed, dancing about, flailing his arms around as if they were detached from his body. The music takes him all around the room. He first dances by his jet black locked chest. He twirls by his desk where his computer rests decorated with multicolored sparkly stickers. The bookshelves above possess a multitude of various trinkets and no books. The rectangular hutch below contains tens of small hand crafted metal figurines. Each was finely painted long ago and naked, rusted metal struggles to peek out, displaying their antiquity.

A giant leap into the air and Jacob passes by a mini version of the Hollywood Sign. Another twirl leads Jacob past his dresser where standing up, hand in hand, are many famous faces of the past, dancing.

Jacob's older brother, Ryan, makes his slow lethargic journey down the hall to Jacob's door, covered in newspaper articles and headlines about Los Angeles. He slowly turns the doorknob and gently pushes the door open. Dancing across his tired eye line is Jacob, still energetic, singing along with the music. Ryan's dead empty stare says something more than exhaustion and frustration. He watches for a moment, remaining silent at the doorway, seeing if Jacob himself would recognize the absurdity of the situation. But there's no chance of that. Jacob is in his own world, his eyes mostly closed, the music notes controlling all of his thoughts and movements, completely taking over his soul.

Ryan shakes his head, reaching a hopeless level of frustration. He slowly lumbers over to the stereo and turns off the music player, silencing Jacob's symphony.

Jacob continues on singing and dancing, blurting out the next set of lyrics, "I love LA!" continuing to flail his arms about. Seconds pass before he realizes the music's been stopped. Confused, Jacob whips his head over to the radio and finds an angry Ryan standing with his arms crossed and a scowl on his face. Ryan's almost too tired to maintain his disapproving stance, with his brows furrowed and his teeth grinding behind his closed lips, portraying his best fatherly pose.

"Good morning, Ryan," Jacob states, grinning—playing the innocent fawn.

"What the hell are you doing?" Ryan shoots at Jacob in disbelief. But as surprised as Ryan is to be standing before his little brother in the early morning, somewhere inside he accepts this as normal Jacob behavior. He enables the absurdity.

Jacob looks surprised, legitimately confused over Ryan's angered demeanor. As if nothing is wrong, Jacob replies to the question posed with a casual, "Dancing."

"It's four AM!" responds Ryan, attempting to reason with his younger brother. He points emphatically at Jacob's plain looking wall clock; probably the only thing ordinary that resides in the colorful room.

Jacob looks over at the clock on his wall. It reads four AM on the dot, just as Ryan said. Jacob removes the giant orange sunglasses from his face and squints, acting as if the clock is much further away than it actually is.

"It's four all right," Jacob agrees.

Ryan glares at Jacob in awe, waiting for an excuse, a comment, a reason why he's gotten up at four AM and danced around in crazy clothes as if he were the village idiot. But there is no distinct reason for his madness, and Ryan is met with silence and a happy-go-lucky smile from Jacob. The two brothers stand before one another, Ryan annoyed, Jacob smiling, for nearly a full minute.

Ryan extends his arms, his face whining, begging, nearly screaming for an answer. A disbelieved grunt is all that falls out of Ryan's mouth.

Jacob remains standing in place, challenging Ryan's parental sanity.

Ryan takes a deep breath, gathering himself and squashing the over-flowing levels of frustration he feels.

"It's early, Jake. It's real early," are all the words Ryan can ramble off without exploding.

"Yeah…I know," Jacob nonchalantly states, again playing the role of the perfect suspect, agreeing to the charges without hesitation but adding no additional information of his own.

Ryan, for the second time, waits for Jacob to elaborate upon his simplistic response. He grows increasingly impatient, his face, arms, chest, legs, and toes all filling with the heat of anger. Ryan bites his tongue just staring at Jacob who maintains his laissez-faire attitude. But that's why Ryan can't be angry. Jacob maintains his innocent expression because he believes he's done nothing wrong. What could a little music and dance hurt?

"Just…" Ryan tries to get out the words but is nearly too frustrated to finish the sentence as he stutters along.

"Just…keep it down." Ryan lets out a deep breath, giving up his futile fight.

"Okay, sure thing Rye," Jacob says, not having a problem in the world.

Ryan shakes his head, running his frustrated hands through his hair. He turns and heads toward the door, muttering angrily to himself. He gently closes the door, still trying to hold all the anger inside. Ryan exhaustedly lumbers down the hallway back towards his bedroom, scratching his head in confusion. It's a walk he has done before.

Jacob peeks his head out into the hallway, watching Ryan lethargically move away. He pulls out a cracked pair of yellow blotch painted binoculars and focuses directly on the back of Ryan's head, seeing nothing but his dark hair. All of a sudden, the back of Ryan's head turns into a white door slamming shut. Jacob flinches back away from his binoculars and disappears back behind his article covered bedroom door.

There is a moment of absolute silence before a re-explosion of music occurs, Jacob starting where the song left off. "I love LA…da-da-da-da…We love it!" Randy Newman shouts throughout the Crestwood household, unaware he's doing anything wrong.

Ryan is sitting on his bed, exhausted, with a blank look on his face. Now, unlike before, he doesn't seem to mind the loud music as much. He casually reaches over to the top drawer of his night stand and pulls out a pair of large thick black headphones. He places them on his head and gently lays his head back down upon his pillow, calmly closing his eyes.

Three

Starktown's Lake Maya is the lone body of water for miles on end. It rests along Thompson Road, a long windy dirt road that stretches from the edge of Starktown all the way across to the rest of the world. William Thompson was a great philanthropist who brought one of John Deere's great farm manufacturing plants into town in the mid1800s. Starktown's economy depended and thrived on the plant until the 1950s. Of course, now, the mill has been torn down, but the lonely dirt road with Thompson's name still remains. And his dirt road is the only decent way to get to Lake Maya.

Maya offers refuge to most of the exotic creatures in town if stray yellow-billed ducks are allowed to be referred to as exotic. Along with the two families of ducks are dozens of bullfrogs who can be heard for miles on end, croaking on cue through the nights. They burrow themselves at the water's edge in some long swaying cattails. The first cattail appeared near the edge of the old girl in the early eighties. Since then, the cattails have made their home at the fingertips of Maya.

The edge of the Shawnee Hills stand just behind Lake Maya and provides a glorious view of the town's great water body. Miles of wheat stand to the east and apple trees to the west. The hills are well forested, covered with a blanket of leaves most of the year. But the leaves have started to fall and the bright yellow, red, and orange dashes of color are popping up amongst the tired green.

A curious small cloud of dust is traveling down the scarcely traveled Thompson Road. Left in the trail of dust is an old wooden sign. The sign's paint and luster have long since gone, small pieces and chips of its body lying on the ground below it. The sign reads: Welcome to Starktown, Illinois, —Pop. 6,584. The population total is like an old little league scoreboard. Each number is removable, black painted digits on dirtied white metal sheets. The last two numbers are crisper and cleaner, as if having been changed within the last few months.

The creator of the dust storm on Thompson is a silver convertible BMW. With its top up, the driver remains a mystery behind the well-tinted windows of the luxury sports car and zooms towards town.

Most of Starktown's roads are cement with a thin layer of dirt sitting on top of the crusty hard surface. The buildings in town are mostly made of wood, some of the newer designs have their walls lined with stucco. Nearly all the buildings are two stories or smaller. The largest building is at the far end of the town, the hospital and resting home. It stands twelve stories high, the town's personal skyscraper, and, at ten years of age, is the most recent addition to Starktown's building community. The automotive presence in town is dominated by pickup trucks. Old rusted and paint-chipped trucks seem to be everywhere. Only the colors and models to keen eyes differentiate one from another.

Trees, small and tall, stand throughout and around the edges of roads in town. They are a welcomed inhibitor in this small, homey world.

The pounding of a few hammers echoes through the quiet neighborhood. In Starktown, the "suburbia" is rural, with some homes separated by two, three, five or even ten acres at times. Some of the townspeople have orchards of apples and peaches, while others live amongst a sea of wheat. The active construction site causing the hammering happens to be on a street just outside of town. It has neighbors within close walking distance, about a hundred feet on either side.

The smacking and banging are coming from a partially built home. It's actually more like the skeleton of a dwelling, as naked pieces of wood beams establish many of the firm roots of the house. The home will be two stories tall, the second barely peeking up above the first. Three hammers at once are pounding on the frame-work of a hand-made dream home in-progress.

"All right, it's chow time!" calls out Ryan Crestwood, leading the small construction team. Not shaken by his early morning rise, Ryan a true rugged blue collar worker, who wears his blue jeans and white t-shirt well.

One by one, the unsynchronized hammering stops.

Stan, tall and uncoordinated, rises to his feet, his ears perking at the sound of lunch. Stan, as far as anyone knows, is almost forty years old. He's lived all his life inside the confines of Starktown and always seems to have a dopey smile on his face, as if he was constantly unsure of what's happening in the world around him. Naturally, Stan is the first to make it over to the back of Ryan's pickup for chow time.

Following closely behind Stan is Martin. Hungry as a horse during his precious feeding hour, Martin rushes excitedly over to the pickup. Sweat is dripping down the sides of his face and his white T-shirt has become soaked with his hours of hard labor in the sun. Three-quarters black, and one-quarter Cuban, Martin's skin has a dark, chocolate shine, glistening with the reflection of the sun from the thin coat of sweat covering his arms and neck. Martin's stout, five-foot eight, nearly two hundred pound frame is longing for a bite of the ham sandwich screaming out his name from inside the large cooler on the flatbed of Ryan's pickup truck.

"Let me at it!" Martin bellows from deep inside his large belly.

Ryan hops up onto his truck and reaches inside a large scratched up red cooler, tossing Stan and Martin beers.

Brown paper lunch bags follow right behind.

"Hey, what's going on here? You guys think you're on a break or somethin'?" asks a sarcastic young Latino voice. Carlos, or 'Los as his friends call him, stands an inch or two below Martin, but those two inches are made up by a fiery personality that features Napoleonesque qualities.

Carlos has a thin mustache and little other signs of facial growth. His golden tan skin is nearly hairless, while his very short black hair stands finely cut with a little flare and spike to it. Carlos's shirt and shorts are Umberto, the world-renown soccer brand clothing line, and the matching outfit, coupled with a gold chain and cross hanging around Carlos's neck, makes him fashionable and cool —at least in his own mind. Carlos struts over to the pickup and Ryan tosses him the last can of beer.

Martin is already tearing apart his ham sandwich, nearly half way done just seconds into lunch time.

"Damn, brother, settle down. Ain't no one taking those slices of pig away from you," Carlos barks sarcastically at Martin.

"Hey, man, you see my stomach? If you're not careful, you'll end up in there too," Martin jokingly jabs back with a mouth full of food.

"You guys are funny," adds Stan dryly, picking at his sloppy hand-made peanut butter and jelly sandwich. Some food accidentally falls out of Stan's mouth, staining his dirty white T-shirt with purple grape jelly. He is by far the dirtiest of all the men working on the site.

"Damn, Stan, you eat worse than the pig that Marty's swallowing right now," adds Carlos, staring at Stan as if he was a disgusting animal.

"Fine!" Stan says. He takes his lunch and, with one bowlegged step after another, stumbles over mounds of choppy dirt to a tree nearby. Stan finds himself on the wrong side of nearly every joke told and today is no different from any other day.

"Now see what you two did?" Ryan, only a little upset, blames Carlos and Martin. He admonishes only because he feels he has to. Ryan and Martin shoot Carlos firm stares with guilt-ridden intentions.

"What?" asks a hot and annoyed Carlos, not wanting to deal with Stan's child-ish antics.

"Come on, 'Los," urges Ryan.

"C'mon," urges Martin, a bit of chewed up ham and bread sneaking out of his full mouth.

"Fine," gives in Carlos. He takes a deep breath and marches over to Stan. Stan, upon recognizing Carlos's presence, turns a cold shoulder, continuing his immature behavior. Carlos shakes his head and gives Stan a friendly smack on the arm. He sits down and the two men eat lunch together, a silent accord reached.

Ryan and Martin smile, amused.

"Anything new?" asks Martin casually, hoping for the slightest bit of exciting news in Ryan's life.

"Nah— same old-same old." Ryan's lackluster response is matched by a subtle level of discomfort about discussing his life.

"Yeah...me too," replies an equally solemn Martin.

"You too? At least you got someone, man. You got a wife. I got a kid bouncing off the walls at my place at 4AM!"

"Shh!" jokingly responds Martin. "Come on man, keep that on the QT. Don't be saying the 'W' word out loud like that."

"You're blessed, man. You got a good loyal wife."

"Yeah...lucky I get yelled at every day of my life. If it's not the toilet seat it's the dishes. How can it be my fault if her behind slides down into the toilet in the middle of the night? All she's gotta do is turn on the light to see the seat's up! I don't even know how her behind fits in that bowl to begin with. She's packin' back there."

"That's what I was gonna ask," jokingly responds Ryan.

"Them are fighting words!" Martin playfully jumps around, his body jiggling up and down, fists in the air.

"Oh, you wanna go now, do ya?" Ryan plays along, also starting to bounce around, raising his hands flamboyantly about, as if he were Muhammad Ali.

"Makin' fun of my woman again!" Martin shouts.

Martin and Ryan lock arms and begin to wrestle, giggling all the while.

Carlos and Stan flash their eyes over to the two grown men who are acting more like twelve year olds.

"Oh, not again," Stan rolls his eyes, not wanting to play along.

"Oh yeah!" jumps up Carlos, excitedly rushing over to be part of the friendly scrap.

Martin and Ryan roll to the ground, each trying to gain the upper hand.

"No way, Big Daddy!" challenges Ryan.

"You mine, little man!" taunts Martin.

"Super Fly!" yells Carlos as he hurls his body on top of Ryan and Martin.

Stan walks over to the three-man free-for-all and eats his sandwich, using the throw-back boyhood bonding moment as entertainment. The men giggle and grab, one trying to get on top of the other.

"Excuse me…" an unrecognizable, angelic voice gently beckons in the crisp adolescent male air. "Excuse me… boys," asks the angelic voice again, coming from street side, an amused tone shining through her gentle interruption.

Stan, with mayonnaise staining the sides of his mouth and bread crumbs handsomely decorating his lips, slowly turns to the street. His mouth drops, awed by a breathtaking sight.

Standing by the driver's side of the silver BMW convertible is Claire. Her posture is that of a feisty fireball, with her arms resting on top of the closed black top of her car. Her soft unblemished skin, the smallest of birthmarks above the upper right corner of her lip, her long curly dark hair—each strand more flowing and wavy than the next —,her inviting, innocent, kind smile, her soft, gentle blue eyes—,seemingly containing an ocean of possibilities, her angelic movements, subtle and graceful, all equate to one glorious word: Claire.

Stan, as if not knowing what to do, nudges the guys on the ground with his foot. "Fellas…hey, fellas," the nervous Stan beckons to his friends needing some help to speak to the beautiful foreign woman.

"So, what's a gal gotta do to get a guy's attention in this town?"

Ryan, Martin, and Carlos all freeze in their odd wrestling poses, looking like deer caught in headlights.

Stan chuckles, amused by the foolishness, but then coughs, choking on some bread crumbs from his sandwich.

While Stan coughs out the crumbs, Ryan, Martin, and Carlos rise to their feet, brushing themselves off.

Claire smiles, making her appearance all the more breathtaking to the adolescent men. "So?" Claire asks with a smirk and a bit of spunk.

"We…we were wrestling…ya know…kinda like how guys sorta do," Ryan states, stammering along.

"You're hot," bluntly blurts out Carlos, staring at Claire as if she were a mythological goddess.

"I'm lookin' for six-twenty Rogers Street and I'm as new as they come in this town. Any compass points you can give me?" poses Claire kindly.

"It's that way," responds Stan candidly, pointing northwest.

Claire smiles, unsure of where that direction might take her.

"What my friend here means, is that if you go to the end of this street and make a right, it's about a block down. I think you wanna go left when ya get there," intelligently answers Martin.

"Excellent. Thanks, fellas." Claire removes her hands off the top of her sleek big-city vehicle and ducks back inside the car.

"Who's your favorite?" Ryan jumps excitedly forward just wanting to make his moments with the mysterious angelic Claire last a moment longer.

Claire peeks her head back above the side of her car and contains a big grin on her face, pondering the question for a moment.

"Your favorite wrestler that is. Who's your favorite wrestler?" reaffirms Ryan, this time a little less jumpy.

Claire thinks for just a moment, entertaining the query.

"I used to like The Rock. I thought he had a cute childlike quality to him. I'd choose him. Later, boys," Claire states with a pleasant raise of her eyebrows. She gets back in her silver BMW and speeds off, leaving a trail of dust in her wake.

All four men are left stunned, shell shocked by a fresh breeze they rarely feel upon their faces.

"She's hot and she knows about wrestling. She's a God," Carlos embellishes.

"Yeah, she sure was something," Ryan says as he stares at the silver machine speeding away, growing smaller and smaller by the second. Claire touched a nerve deep inside Ryan, a chord that had not been rung in a long while. In an instant, Ryan is tackled from the side, Martin taking him down to the ground. Soon after, Carlos flies on top of the dog pile, the three adolescent men returning to their previous activity.

Stan stares at the melee, itching to join the brouhaha this time. "What the heck," Stan says to himself, and he too jumps on top of the pile. The four men roll around on the ground, laughing and giggling like they were back in elementary school.

Four

Howard Stevenson owns the local pub in town. After a long day of work, there is nothing like kicking back a cold one at Howie's Pub.

The bar didn't look like much from outside, just a quaint joint with a dirt parking lot. Old strings of white small lights, like the ones folks use during holiday times, hang around the gutters of the old tavern. The windows give a taste of the décor inside, with florescent beer signs making themselves visible to any and all who roam by.

The pub inside is not that much different than its simple homey exterior. The stench of stale peanuts and scuzzy beer fills the air. The aroma isn't overwhelming, but strangely inviting. The dim lighting creates a relaxing, kickback tone.

Classic rock supplied by an old fifties jukebox subtly sends out Bob Marley's "No Woman, No Cry," its electric notes making their way throughout the entire bar. A feeling of closeness and familiarity strikes all who enter the small town establishment.

Guss Walters, a seventy-five year old townie, always seems to be at the second stool. He clears his throat every hour on the hour. Guss chomps on his bowl of beer nuts as he watches the Fighting Illini battle the Hoosiers on the hard court on one of the three televisions.

The cue ball strikes the seven ball flush, knocking it cleanly into the right corner pocket. Martin, Ryan, Stan, and Carlos are kicking back playing pool in the rear of the bar.

"Yes!" exclaims Martin. "That's the way you get the groove on, baby," Martin, holding a cue stick, celebrates his near professional pool skills by showing off his not-so-nearly professional dance skills. He grooves, slowly shaking his hips, first to the right, then back to left.

"All right, big boy, let's see those skills again," challenges Ryan, anxiously holding his pool stick, waiting for his turn.

"Here you go, boys," proclaims the deep, scruffy voice of Howard Stevenson. His voice takes on the complexion of a pirate more so than a tender a of bar in a small town. But he wears the look of Starktown well. He's short, stout, and mostly bald, with short fringes of hair seemingly tracking further and further back on his head with each day that passes. Stevenson sets down a tray of four monogrammed glasses, each containing a rough riding cowboy on his buck, and a giant pitcher of beer fit for four thirsty men.

"Thanks, Haas," collectively responds the four friends.

Stan grabs the pitcher to pour the beers but is immediately met by 'Los's hands. "No-no," states Carlos. "Remember…you lost your pouring privileges last time."

"That's right, no glass, Stan. You know the rules," reminds Ryan.

Stan shrugs and pouts like a five year old that just got scolded, sitting his butt back down on his seat. He watches as Carlos fills the four cold glasses with the frosty thick potion of wheat, barley, and suds.

"Ha-ha! I love it! I love it!" Martin cocky, shouts with exuberance watching as the eight ball he just knocked slowly but surely rolls towards the winning corner pocket. But as if a fate jumped up and slightly tipped the table, the eight ball fades left and lips the pocket, sitting on the edge of the hole. Martin uses every muscle in his body, attempting to telepathically cause the eight to fall, but it does not. It sits firmly over the edge of the hole, the painted eight staring back at Martin, mocking him. "No! Oh…damn!" complains Martin. He scours, prematurely accepting the bitter taste of defeat. A scream, a cough, the passing of gas, any of these actions could cause the ball to fall into the hole, less than an inch separating the ball from the hole.

Ryan licks his chops, smiling at Martin. Ryan picks up a block of blue chalk and begins to gently rub the tip of his stick. Only two balls remain on the table, the cue and the eight ball. The taste of victory is thick in Ryan's salivating mouth. "Ya know, that lady looked pretty smart," Ryan randomly blurts out.

"Smart?" chuckles Martin.

"Sounds like somebody's got it bad for the Beamer-babe," jokes Carlos.

"Yeah...I think she was smart, too," adds Stan seriously, excited to join the conversation.

Carlos and Martin shake their heads at Stan, disregarding his weak addition to the conversation. As usual, Stan is unable to keep the momentum of the male bonding session going.

"You think she's gonna stick around?" asks Ryan curiously.

"Damn, you do got it bad," jokes Carlos again. "Stop dragging this out," demands Martin impatiently, not wanting his imminent defeat to linger any longer than it has to.

"All right," Ryan smirks and prepares himself to take the easy shot. He leans across the table, focusing behind the cue ball. He slides the stick smoothly through his fingers, back and forth, continuing to aim the shot down. He slides it back for the final time, readying to strike the ball.

Just then, the small bell attached to the bar door jingles.

Ryan, distracted, mis-hits the ball and lips the hole firmly, completely missing the eight ball, sending the cue ball back across the table. Martin's eyes widen with excitement as Ryan's face drops with frustration.

"Oh, bad luck," sarcastically comments Stan.

But the cue ball continues on, lipping the far corner. And as if guided back to the hole by a transmitter, the cue ball continues back towards the eight ball.

"No way!" Carlos shouts, stepping up closer to the table, his eyes growing with anticipation of the unintentional circus shot.

"No!" whines Martin.

Ryan's expression and demeanor have also changed. He's excited as he watches the cue ball steadily approach the eight ball. He moves with the ball, tracking it across the table, his face straining, begging for it to continue on. It rolls right up to the eight, slowing as it reaches it. A gentle kiss from the cue to the eight, and the black ball, with all of a centimeter of movement, drops into the hole.

"Yes!" shouts Ryan, pumping his fist up into the air.

"Oh, what kind of crap is that!" shouts Martin in protest. "Again the black man gets robbed by the white man!" Martin shouts, joking, but still with his pouty, overly competitive face.

"Hey…looks like you got lucky twice," says Carlos, staring at the front of the bar where Claire stands casually.

Claire, once again, is wearing a professional outfit, looking striking in her red power suit.

"Don't worry, my brother, I'll set the mood for you. I got your back," declares Martin as he rests his arm on Ryan's shoulder, the two of them staring at Claire.

Standing by the solid oak bar, Claire calmly twiddles her fingers, panning her eyes across the different colorful signs. Old man Walters breaks his trance on the basketball game and makes eye contact with Claire. She smiles kindly at Guss, the only response she'd ever give to a stranger, and like a light switch getting flipped on, his face lights up and he grins. Guss displays his half a mouthful of brown chompers to Claire. His dried wrinkled scruffy face lifts up a bit, a smile breaking through his permanent grimace.

From a distance, Ryan continues to watch Claire like a hawk, holding his breath for her next move. The angelic figure says something to Stevenson that causes the two of them to smile. Ryan can feel the butterflies charged up inside his belly. He's like a nervous school boy. Claire's obviously a big-city girl and he's just a townie. The pressure is mounting.

"Come on, what are you waiting for? You're a stud, man. You're a love machine!" encourages Carlos, trying to motivate Ryan anyway he can.

"Yeah…you got a great caboose working for ya," adds Stan.

"Just be quiet. You're not helping," Carlos scolds Stan.

"All right…I'm going in," the less than confident Ryan says.

Martin jumps around, excited. He rushes over to the jukebox, nearly giddy to pick a song for his good friend.

"Okay…okay…everything's gonna be cool," Ryan tries to remind himself, slowly but surely losing whatever motivation and confidence he had with each step he takes toward Claire.

Martin shoves his two quarters into the jukebox and immediately sees the song selection he wants. He has a sinister grin on his face as he pushes the code in. Vanilla Ice's "Ice, Ice, Baby" blasts through the bar. The song brings smiles to everyone around. Martin displays what little hip hop dancing his body can handle, spinning and laughing, having a great time with the gag.

Claire turns toward the jukebox, also amused by the song. She nearly turns right into Ryan. Ryan's head is turned back at Martin, mumbling angry thoughts about his good friend who gives him a thumbs up, as the big man dances back over to Stan and Carlos.

"So…you choose this catchy tune?" asks the sweet voice of Claire.

Ryan whips his head back around and gulps, caught off-guard by Claire. He stares at her, speechless, unsure of what to say.

"Let me guess, you were preparing something witty in mind but the coolness of Vanilla Ice threw you off?" Claire asks playfully.

"Something like that," Ryan flashes his pearly whites, settling down a bit. "This seat taken?"

"Go ahead," Claire says, giving Ryan a subtle head nod and allowing him to take the seat next to her.

Guss Walters looks annoyed by Ryan swooping in, any glimmer of the old man's misguided hopes of sitting with Claire dissipating before his eyes. He sports a grimace and goes back to watching his basketball, tossing a handful of nuts back into his mouth.

Stevenson sets down a couple of beers in front of the budding couple, giving Ryan a quick wink and nod, wishing him luck.

"Thanks, Haas."

"Haas, huh?" asks Claire curiously, looking at Ryan with a grin. "You probably know everybody in this place right now."

Ryan takes a quick peek around the bar, seeing his three immature friends gawking at two of them. "Yep...I know them all," he says, reluctant to take credit for everyone in the bar.

There is a moment of uncomfortable silence as the two of them sip their beers. Thoughts are racing through Ryan's head, trying to think of something—anything—witty to say. But he's drawing blanks. With each second that goes by, the silence grows more and more uncomfortable.

"So...ya come here often?" the cheesy question rolls off Ryan's tongue, the angst on his face displaying how much he hates himself at this moment.

Claire looks at Ryan with a half-cocked smile, the question not exactly earth-shattering. "I'm just off the boat, remember?"

"That's right. That wasn't the smartest question I've ever asked," responds Ryan, feeling lower and lower, as he digs a deeper hole for himself.

"What was the most interesting question you've ever asked?" poses an interested Claire, showing a bit of her spunk.

"Huh?" asks Ryan, again caught off-guard by Claire.

"I'll go first. The most interesting question I've ever asked in my life…hmmm…let me see," Claire thinks to herself.

"Wow, she's gorgeous," Ryan thinks to himself, his breath taken away by Claire's beauty.

"I think the most interesting question I ever asked someone was: 'are you happy?'" Claire stares at Ryan with a wide-eyed optimism and excitement that invigorates the soul of the small town construction worker. Claire continues to stare at Ryan, waiting for an answer.

"Oh…you mean me?" responds Ryan.

"Yeah. Are you happy? I ask because I believe the way a person answers the simplest of questions tells a lot about them."

"Simple maybe on the surface, but a lot more complex inside," responds Ryan deeply, now completely submersed inside the conversation, free of the nervousness that had previously haunted him.

Claire smiles, appreciating Ryan's depth. "I'm Claire," she contently responds, convinced of Ryan's sincerity, depth, and intelligence. She leaves her right hand extended for Ryan to take.

"I'm Ryan Crestwood. It's a pleasure to meet you, Claire." Ryan accepts Claire's offer of introduction and the two shake hands.

Back by the pool tables, the boys' locker room lifts up with excitement. "That's right, baby! Our boy's in the house!" excitedly comments Martin, he and the other three schoolboys watching closely.

"He got some skin. That a baby!" Carlos also shows some exuberance.

"I don't think it looks good," comments Stan negatively.

"Shut-up, Stan!" Martin and Carlos say in tandem.

Claire and Ryan share a moment, the two of them sipping their suds while staring into each other's eyes. There's a feeling of home between them, an unexplainable natural closeness.

"You like our little town?" poses Ryan.

"It's not so bad. I didn't see any Starbucks though. I'll definitely miss that," answers Claire candidly.

"But ya know, there's some level of comfort in knowing your neighbors. It's nice," Ryan delivers the line with a sense of warmth.

"It's amazing…two totally different worlds separated by a few miles of roads and fields," Claire philosophizes. They each take another sip of their brew, but this time they're not stalling, they're just thirsty.

"So, what does a guy like you do for a living in this small town?"

"Construction," Ryan says. "I've always been really good with my hands," he casually states to Claire as if he legitimately has a gift and is, totally unaware of its double meaning. Claire smiles, looking down to the ground, momentarily unable to look Ryan in the eyes. She takes the sexual meaning beyond its innocent words.

Ryan is confused, thinking for a second, unsure of what was so funny about what he said. He realizes what he said and his eyes flare open and he starts to shake his head.

"It's okay. It was funny," she replies.

"So…what do you do?" Ryan returns, trying to return the conversation back on the smooth track, changing subjects as quickly as possible.

"Interior design," Claire replies. Something strikes her and she glances at her watch, seizing this moment to end the pleas and conversation. "Hey, Haas…"

Stevenson, drying a glass with a white towel, looks up with a half-cocked smile, enjoying Claire's use of his local nickname.

"Your clock on the wall right?"

Stevenson looks behind him at the clock reading six-thirty. "Yep, as far as I know, it's right to the second," confidently states Stevenson, his grin fading away as he goes back to drying glasses.

"Gotta go," Claire declares to Ryan, gathering herself to leave.

Ryan becomes panicked, caught by surprise over Claire's sudden change of heart.

"Can I see you sometime?" Ryan rushes the words out of his mouth with an air of desperation in his voice.

"It's a small town…remember? I'll see you soon. I'm pretty sure of it," Claire states with little urgency, confident she will probably see this kind, handsome, small town innocent sometime in the near future. "Thanks for the company. See ya." Claire waves casually as she exits the bar.

"Yeah…see ya," Ryan responds helplessly.

Ryan searches the bar counter for his pride, but finds nothing but the rings of condensation left where their beers once stood. Ryan catches his breath, perplexed. He tries to gather himself, first by downing the remains of his beer. "Way to go, stud," Ryan compliments himself sarcastically. He makes brief mental preparations for the barrage of questioning he's about to face from his friends and rises from his bar stool, taking the long walk back over to the pool table where the piranhas anxiously wait. Ryan walks up to the silent trio who are waiting for some expression, a clue of what went on. Ryan calmly raises his head and looks his three friends over, expressionless, as if he hadn't just met the girl of his dreams and watched her walk away. "Whose shot is it?"

"Whose shot is it? That's all we get?" complains Martin.

"Come on, Ryno, what's the word?" begs Carlos. "You going home with her?" guesses Stan excitedly, wanting something dirty to happen.

"She already left, you tool!" Carlos insults Stan, tired of his senseless comments.

"What happened, man?" calmly urges Martin, wanting the inside scoop.

"Got a number?" tosses out Carlos, continuing the assault of questions.

"What's her name? She looks like a Laura. I like the name Laura," Stan says to himself, going off into his own little world of thought.

"Her name's Claire. She's…incredible. I didn't get her number. I…I was going to but just when I got around to asking her out, she left."

What do you mean, she left?" poignantly asks Martin.

"She asked me what I did. I told her construction," Ryan says, his friends closely listening, not yet seeing any flaws in the conversation. "And I said…"

"What—what?" Carlos asks, desperate to know. "What'd you say?" Martin, acting like an excited curious school girl, beckons.

"I told her I was in construction…that I've always been good with my hands," Ryan runs his hands over his face, knowing he may have inadvertently insulted Claire with a sleazy pick-up line.

There is a moment of silence as, Martin, Carlos, and Stan digest Ryan's conversation snippet.

"That's our boy!" shouts Martin with vigor, laughing and congratulating Ryan.

"That's the Ryno we know!" asserts Carlos, laughing too.

"She must have thought I was an ass."

"No, she probably thought you just wanted a piece of her ass," Stan jokes.

Ryan shoots Stan a sneer, not amused by his comment.

"That's better, baby!" Carlos commends Stan on his successful stab at Ryan, giving him a friendly punch in the arm. Stan smiles, proud of himself, and then holds his arm in pain from the jab.

"That's too funny, man…Awesome, baby…I can't believe you didn't tell her you could give her some sugar…," the voices of all his friends blend and fade together into one collective unrecognizable blurb in the back of Ryan's head. Instead, his concentration is on the bar door by which Claire exited just moments before. He gazes at it, knowing deep inside that he just came across someone very special; someone that stirred his insides with dozens of dancing butterflies.

Five

Another day passes by in Starktown. The sun is slowly being dragged down below the horizon, darkness beginning to consume the town. Within minutes, the wondrous red and purple streaks reflecting upon a few stratus blend into the face of night. The sky struggles vigorously to hold on to its light which is fleeing away by the second.

The sporadic melodies of crickets begin to fill the atmosphere all around, officially orchestrating the start of evening.

An owl hoots, hidden amongst the thick branches of a mighty oak.

Ryan's old trusty red pickup comes bouncing and creaking into the driveway of the Crestwood household. He lethargically exits his truck, dragging from a long day of work and play. He picks up his beat-up cooler in the back of the truck and carries it along with his tired bones over to the front door. He struggles to hold the cooler while taking the keys out of his pocket. The cooler slips and falls to the ground, bouncing off of Ryan's left foot.

"Darnit!" shouts Ryan, hopping for a second on his good foot. He shakes his head, frustrated and tired with life. He inserts his house key and gently pushes open the front door. He reaches down and grabs the cooler, stepping into his quiet, comforting home. He closes the door behind him and hears a strange rolling sound. It sounds like wheels tracking across the back of the house from left to right. The rolling increases in volume as it moves towards the entrance where Ryan is standing. Ryan barely blinks an eye, familiar with the unusual noise approaching him. He takes a deep breath, attempting to unleash some of his frustrations, preparing for an even more frustrating evening.

The rolling turns into a near thunderous pitch as Jacob comes flying around the corner of the living room dressed in full hockey gear with of course, accompanying roller blades. His Los Angeles Kings jersey hangs loosely on his thin frame. Oddly, instead of a hockey helmet, Jacob is wearing an old Los Angeles Raiders football helmet—, the colors, silver and black, matching his Los Angeles Kings jersey. Multiple black knee and elbow pads decorate the arms and legs of Jacob for, a total of twelve, three surrounding each joint. Oversized stark white hockey gloves stretch half way up Jacob's arms, nearly kissing the black elbow pads.

Jacob smiles and waves as he passes by an annoyed Ryan. He rolls right by the staircase, disappearing around the corner. Ryan cracks a brief but amused smile, releasing a little of his tension. He shakes his head, takes a deep breath, and waits, as the rolling thunder distantly moves from the back of the house, and charges back around toward the front. The rolling blades far proceed Jacob's actual presence as he gets closer and closer to another lap. Jacob stumbles along as he peeks around the corner, balancing himself with his arms spread wide like a bird's wings.

"It's poker night!" shouts Ryan, trying to rush the words out of his mouth as quickly as possible to communicate with his fleet-footed brother.

"Cooooool!" responds Jacob, his voice fading as he again wraps around the corner, disappearing from Ryan's sight line.

Ryan rolls his neck, the tension again beginning to build, growing impatient with Jacob's roller blading. Ryan waits, now setting the cooler down at his feet and sitting on top of its cover. The rolling thunder once again comes charging around the living room, back to the front of the house where Ryan anxiously awaits his younger brother.

"Just one week out of school and you're already driving me crazy," Ryan speaks out-loud to himself, venting his frustration.

Jacob jumps one hundred and eighty-degrees around and rolls shakily backwards, turning his head to see where he's going.

Ryan hops up to his feet and grabs the cooler, cradling it with his arms. He presses up against the front door, making his body as little of an obstacle as possible.

"You gonna stay upstairs?" again rushes Ryan's voice, wanting to be heard.

"Don't know!" shouts Jacob, his voice flexing more as he nearly loses his balance yet again.

Jacob does another one hundred and eighty-degree turn just before he curves around the corner. He clips the wall, stomping his blades to gain balance. Jacob rears his butt back and continues to blade off to the other side of the house.

Ryan lets out a breath of frustrated air and runs his hands through his hair. He looks on the wall behind him where rolled up elastic bands are wound tight at chest and knee level. Ryan struggles to hold the cooler with just his left hand and grabs the higher elastic band and pulls it out. He pulls it to the banister on the staircase where two small black circular holsters reside. The elastic band is not unlike that which you might find at a local movie theater, or an amusement park: bands used to herd people like sheep to their desired destination.

The rolling thunder once again advances upon Ryan and there's Jacob, speeding around the living room. Ryan quickly latches the elastic band into its holster and jumps back.

Jacob sees the band stretched across his path at chest level and a competitive smile emerges on his face. His eyes flare open with excitement and he drops down on his right knee so that it's nearly touching the ground. Jacob rolls right underneath the chest high elastic band and sneaks by, victoriously smiling and waving at Ryan.

Ryan shakes his head in disgust. He again sets down the cooler, letting out a deep sigh of frustration. He takes the elastic band, still rolled up at knee level, and stretches it across to the staircase banister. He successfully attaches the elastic band, now placing his body behind both stretched out bands, guaranteeing the end to Jacob's continuous blading. Ryan crosses his arms, satisfied he will stop his younger brother.

Jacob once again sling-shots around the wall of the living room. Jacob doesn't slow down, continuing to gain in speed. He eyes Ryan firmly, as if encouraging a possible collision.

Ryan swallows, growing a little nervous. Jacob's speeding towards the elastic bands with no end in sight. Then, at the last moment, Jacob suddenly screeches to a halt, stopping just short of the 'band-barricade'.

Ryan lets out the air he's been anxiously holding in his lungs.

"Yes?" asks Jacob casually, breathing heavily in his football helmet with beads of sweat over his happy-go-lucky smile.

"You need me to drive you to the DVD store?" asks Ryan, wanting to deter Jacob from hanging around during the card game.

Jacob pauses for a moment, thinking to himself. "I think I'll play tonight," returns a confident and certain Jacob.

"Really?" responds a surprised and unenthusiastic Ryan.

"Yeah…why not?" Jacob poses.
"You do know that we use real money," Ryan tries to deter his brother.

"Well, I should hope so," Jacob responds, expecting nothing less of the late night gambling excursion.

"Okay," Ryan reluctantly accepts his younger brother's wishes, unsure of what this might mean later on. The two remain standing before each other, each brother staring back into the eyes of the other. Jacob looks as if he might have something to say, his lips subtly twitching in an odd way. Ryan waits, and waits, and waits, but gets nothing from Jacob who just remains staring right back at him like a mirror.

"What?" Ryan explodes with confusion and curiosity.

Jacob rolls his eyes down to the elastic bands. His eyes speak volumes, demanding Ryan to unlatch the same elastic bands he used to temporarily jail his younger brother.

"Oh," Ryan unlatches first the top elastic band, and it whips back to the wall. He then unlatches the bottom and it too snaps right back. Ryan steps to the side and Jacob races by, again rolling around the house.

"Woo!" yells Jacob exuberantly, bursting with excitement to continue his indoor blading display.

Ryan shrugs off his zealous younger brother and carries his cooler upstairs with him. He walks up the creaking stairs and heads down the hallway, disappearing into the bedroom, quietly closing the door behind him. Ryan leaves no trace of his existence, silent as a mouse inside his bedroom.

A large silver and black football helmet sticks out from behind the stairway wall, the face slowly and carefully peering up the stairs towards Ryan's bedroom. Jacob curiously looks to see if Ryan is still around. But there is no sign of Ryan. Satisfied he's now alone, Jacob shoves off with about a tenth of the enthusiasm he had before. He rolls ever so methodically along the slick wood floor, continuing his path around the house, now just gliding along. It seems some of the fun has faded.

A thick mist of smoke and the scent of numerous musty stogies encompass the atmosphere of the Crestwood living room.

The bells of the oak-laced century old grandfather clock toll ten times. It stands grandly by itself in a corner of the living room. The room, as a whole, is a stark reminder of the Crestwood house of old with a splash of the new. Its antiquities have collected dust, almost as if it is a tomb buried deep below soft Egyptian soil. There are framed photos of Jacob and Ryan from their younger days. Hidden in the shadows of the room is a twenty-four inch television, maybe seven to eight years old. Resting on top of the television is an equally old DVD/VCR combo player flashing 10:00…10:00…10:00…over and over again. A hand-knit rug with tens of small red flowers and tiny yellow buds, each with green stems, are spread about the ground amongst an off-white back-drop. Equally off-white is the sofa, which has been moved off to the side of the room along with two of its end tables. Each glossed oak end table has an old plain lamp set atop them, the base, body, and shade all various tones of brown, all of which blend together into the epitome of plainness.

"This hand's smokin'!" Martin pronounces with a sinister cackle behind his voice. "Two dollars," demands Martin with the utmost confidence. He flips two blue chips into an all-American pot, the chips red, white, and blue. They rest easy in the center of the velvet green gambling circle. The green felt table contains five intense players, each resting their laurels upon five brown folding chairs watching a vastly growing pot and tension builds in the room.

Ryan, Martin, Carlos, and Stan, all seriously surveying their cards, are dressed in flannel long sleeve shirts and jeans. It's like a mountain-man convention. Jacob is wearing an oversized black Styrofoam cowboy hat and giant black clown sunglasses. A teal button-down shirt and black and white checkered pants complete Jacob's outrageous ensemble. The ear-to-ear grin on Jacob's face is complemented by a large mound of chips—by far the most of any of the players.

"Damn, two bucks!" contemplates Carlos, momentarily glancing down at his regrettably scarce pile of chips. He ponders the decision, straining as the seconds go by as if the two blue chips representing a mere two dollars were the button to launch nuclear missiles. A near sweat has broken out on Carlos's face as a puff of smoke encompasses his thoughts, kindly sent over by Martin, reaffirming his position of strength and confidence.

"No...," mumbles Carlos. "No!" he says again, definitively. "I'm out," Carlos reluctantly gives in, letting out a gasp of deep-rooted tension built up by this decision making process, tossing his cards into the pot.

"Sure, why not?" casually comments Stan without a thought. Stan tosses two of his blue chips in, matching Martin's initial bet.

"Jesus, do you at least have a decent hand?" barks Ryan at Stan irritably, questioning his poker savvy while at the same time questioning his own hand.

"Maybe," Stan responds, like a child hiding a secret.

"You can't bluff when other people have already bet!" Ryan continues with his reign of Grinchness.

"I'm doin' just fine," Stan, now with the utmost assurance smoothly presents.

"Just let him play his own hand. He's a big boy," chimes in Martin, his greedy eyes seeing the dollar signs.

"What...you got a good hand over there, player?" Ryan beckons Martin, growing more and more paranoid as the game intensifies.

"You guys always talk this much when you play?" inquires a relaxed Jacob to the tense foursome. Jacob doesn't even display the mere impression of being nervous, but why should he? The stack of chips sitting before him is equal to the four other men's stacks combined.

Martin lets out a sinister, cocky cackle, amused by Jacob's innocence and glimmer of common sense.

Ryan shakes his head, disregarding all comments and actions around him, becoming nearly incensed over the consistently defeatist flavor his evening has been marred with. Ryan angrily grabs his last two blue chips and tosses them into the swelling pot, begging for a hand to come his way.

The attention of the table turns to Jacob. He fixes his giant black sunglasses with his right hand, straightening them out. Then, with two chips already boldly clinched in his left hand, Jacob halfheartedly flips them into the pot. A silent self-assurance circumscribes Jacob's expression, remaining valiant and sharp, the ideal stoic poker face.

Martin, bursting with enthusiasm, lays his cards down, face up for the world to see. "Check it out!" he encourages. His three aces over two tens stands tall and firm as a nearly unbeatable top-of-the-line full house.

"Nice," compliments Carlos, thankful he didn't try and compete with Martin's awesome display.

"Dammit!" shouts a resentful and exasperated Ryan, hurling his cards down at the pot.

"Oh," Stan mumbles with a taste of confusion. His eyes are moving back and forth between his concealed hand and Martin's ace-high boat.

"Fess up, man," Carlos curiously urges, wanting to see Stan's hand.

Stan proudly lays his hand down on the table. Two kings, an eight of hearts, a jack of diamonds, and a two of clubs. There's a moment of silence as everyone looks Stan's cards over in disbelief of their futility. "There must be something more" is the general mindset as the eight pairs of eyes pan back and forth over what is simply "'kings.'" Stan smiles, the foolish grin of a child.

"A pair of kings? A pair of kings?!" shouts Ryan at Stan, exploding with thwarting and bafflement. "You went against three other people with a pair of kings?" repeats

Ryan, dwelling in a much more controlled, saddened, almost begging, tone.

Carlos consults Stan's ignorance with a condescending pat on the shoulder. "I really thought you had him, man," comments 'Los sarcastically.

"Thanks, brother," replies the totally oblivious Stan, missing the absurd lack of sincerity whirling around him. Martin is salivating over the pot, completely cued in on what he knows to be his.

"Whatcha got, Jake?" asks Carlos.

Martin's head snaps over to Jacob, the smile fleeing, and for now, the drool over dollar signs seizing. A glitter of concern is dashed over Martin's victory parade. He holds his breath, his face frozen in anticipation of Jacob's response.

The smoky room waits intensely on Jacob's deliberate answer, as he peers through his thick black oversized spectacles.

"Are all of them in a row good?" Jacob calmly and innocently asks.

"Good, but a straight doesn't stand a chance against my monster boat!" Martin, again self-assured, simultaneously relaxes and relishes in his apparent victory. He reaches his greedy hands out to grab the pot. "Come to papa."

Jacob lies his hand down on the table, showing off a ten, jack, queen, king, and ace…all in the suit of spades. "Shucks, and they looked so good together, them all being the same color and all," Jacob comments, as if he didn't know he won.

Everyone stares at the royal flush in a messiah-like manner.

"Holy crap!" states the outspoken Carlos in shock over Jacob's cards.

Martin's greedy smile flips upside down in shock. His hands, surrounding the pot, also freeze, equally stunned by what his eyes are witnessing.

"Jake, that's a royal flush!" a stunned and empathetic Ryan asserts to his brother. He looks in awe at the cards and then back up at Jacob, checking to see if he recognizes the magnitude of his Goliath hand.

Martin's head drops, sinking down to the table, feebly hiding his face in his thick tree branch arms.

"I win?" asks Jacob, playing dumb.

"Yeah, you win…big time, man," Carlos cues Jacob in on the happenings.

Jacob reaches out and collects all his winnings, a subtle and brief sophisticated smile flashing by his face. It's the look of a predator that just matter-of-factly attacked and tore apart its prey.

Ryan, proudly puffing his stogie as if he himself won, swaggers behind Martin. Ryan struggles to hold his laughter back, nearly busting up in front of his best friend, wanting so badly to kick him while he's down. But instead, Ryan pats Martin on the shoulders, more than happy to play the role of consoler to his good buddy.

"I can't believe he pulled a royal flush," Martin slowly raises his head in amazement.

"Yeah, your ace-high boat was lookin' pretty good," Stan states the obvious.

Martin glares at Stan, not amused by his commentary. "Yeah Stan, it sure beats a pair of kings," Martin bitterly mutters back.

"It's all part of poker," mumbles Ryan, his cigar taking up the right side of his mouth while the smoke seeps out.

"This game's turning ugly and I'm kinda tired anyway. I think I'll cash in," proclaims Jacob.

"What did he say?" asks Carlos, in shock over Jacob's sudden declaration.

"Hell, no!" Martin erupts, still angry over his bitter defeat. He scowls at Ryan, attempting to appeal to his poker senses.

"Just let the kid go," Stan randomly suggests to the disgust of his other three co-workers.

"Quiet Stan!" Ryan snapping at his dumb-witted friend. "Look Jacob…," Ryan refocuses, calming himself down. "In poker, it's not polite to quit while you're so far ahead without giving us some kind of warning," Ryan says, continuing to rationalize the situation with his less experienced brother.

"Yeah, it's about fairness, ya know?" adds Carlos, also seeking to reason with Jake.

"Let me see if I understand you guys…you want me to let you win your money back?" Jacob poses, confused over this unspoken rule.

Martin lets out a gasp. "Well, when you put it that way, it sounds kinda stupid," realizing Jacob's point, scratching the top of his head with little more to add.

"No, what we mean is, you gotta give us some kind of warning…or something," Ryan expresses as if there was an established guide to poker etiquette. The four men lean in, hoping, begging Jacob to play himself out of his winnings. Jacob pauses, as if considering their offer. The tension in the air is cutting the thick mist of smoke.

"Being a mere rookie…" Jacob begins. "A virginal player if you will, at this so-called sport or game that you've all so skillfully excelled at, I'd have to say the rules of common sense overwhelm me, and regretfully, persuade me to retire, even though I greatly appreciate and understand each and every one of your positions," states Jacob, as if he were a congressmen.

"Huh?" asks Martin, all the men collectively perplexed by Jacob's explosion of literal eloquence.

"I'm cashin' out," Jacob presents simply to the laymen sitting around him. He rises from the table and respectfully tips the front of his giant Styrofoam hat. "You all have a good evening, now," Jacob states as if he were a cowboy from the old west. He then removes his hat, sliding all the chips over the giant brim, filling up the absurd head gear. He casually moves away from the table, expressionless, and without a word to anyone. Jacob's silence is bold and confident, but not meant to be cocky.

The four men who just got schooled by a teenager playing poker for the first time are left catatonic; stunned in their seats. They each glance down at their puny pile of chips and scratch their heads, wondering what just hit them.

As midnight approached in Starktown, only two men remained at the Crestwoods. Ryan and Martin, each with a bottle of half-drunken beer in their hands, are gently swaying back and forth on two rocking chairs. They're staring off the porch out into the dark silent night. Martin glances at his watch, checking the time, knowing full well his wife has him on a strict curfew.

"So, what's it like to go home to somebody every night?" Ryan asks, as if the thought had been dangling on his tongue for hours.

"Where did that come from?" Martin returns with a curious smile.

"You'll be going home tonight, or any other night for that matter, and you got someone there; someone to cook for you, care for you, to worry about how you're feeling and what you're thinking. That's not so bad," Ryan shares intimately.

"You haven't had to eat her food," Martin jokes sarcastically, wanting to break the sense of drama surrounding Ryan's thoughts. Martin chuckles for just a moment as he watches Ryan project a friendly smile that quickly fades away.

"What do you like most about your marriage?" Ryan remains serious and focused, his curiosity getting the best of him.

"Seriously?" Martin recognizes Ryan's solemn mannerisms and pensive glare.

"Yeah, serious," Ryan replies genuinely, anxious to hear Martin's response.

"Okay," Martin thinks, taking Ryan's question to heart, seriously pondering his response. "What I like most?" Martin reposes the question to himself. "I like that she knows how to touch me. Not…ya know," Martin referring to intimate touching. "But just holding my hand and gently caressing the sides of my face…or how she scratches my neck and rubs my ears. I really like that stuff. It's like a silent way of her saying she loves me without ever speaking a single word," Martin sits deep in his own thoughts and kind memories. A glossy smile is plastered across his face until he realizes he's a man drinking a beer with his best friend. The smile flees and becomes more serious. "Stuff like that," he says, and then takes a sip of his man brew.

"You like that ear rubbing thing?" questions Ryan.

Martin reviews the question carefully, not wanting to look unmanly or too sensitive. "Yeah," he projects firmly, standing strong by his original comments. "It's nice," he adds.

"Yeah, I like that too…the ear thing. It's cool," Ryan agrees.

"It's cool, baby," Martin jokes.

Martin and Ryan laugh, each drinking their beers, the conversation coming to an end on a lighter note.

Six

At the edge of the Shawnee, resting above a quiet and calm Lake Maya, lays the massive body of a grown man. His tall, broad body spans a healthy six feet four inches. He's surrounded by a sea of tall grass and dancing yellow lilies. The deep darkened clouds dominate the sky above. But something is amiss. The clouds are moving at speeds far greater than normal, collectively whisking their massive bodies through the sky.

The seemingly unconscious man comes to; his large fingers bend ever so slightly, stretching back and forth, as if they hadn't been used in some time. They are the hands of a working man, perhaps a lumberjack or a craftsman.

Many calluses and small scars decorate the well-worked fingers and palms of the man's rugged hands.

A deep rolling thunder shakes the earth, momentarily causing the world to tremble. An intensely unsettling chill sets in as the wind blows more fiercely. One by one, the bright yellow buds wilt off the sporadically growing lilies, their tiny arms breaking away. The wind carries the brown wilted buds off into nothingness.

The large man, a pillar of strength, sits up, his face carved by life. Imprints of time have been left all over the man's skin. A two-inch scar streaks across his chin, maybe from chicken wire or a fall when he was a youth. His gray eyes are surrounded by lines of time, crinkling off in all directions like rays off the sun. The strong and sturdy man peers around, his sad gray eyes glazed with a disturbance unbeknownst to himself. His fine dark hair rests gently upon his head, undisturbed by Mother Nature's breath.

A single cardinal takes flight, its healthy dark red coat stained dramatically against the gloomy gray canvas in the sky. A serene flight by a serene bird as it glides through the air as if it were a wondrous summer day.

The man is star-struck by the graceful creature, watching it ever so closely as it flies higher and higher, rising towards the low grey ceiling above. And in an instant, the cardinal in its gentle flight pierces a thick dark cloud, disappearing into the belly of the giant dark pillows above. A single orphaned feather dances down from the angels, riding back and forth towards the ground in the firm breeze.

The man extends his rugged and scarred left hand and catches the fallen feather in his palm. He carefully inspects its beauty and subtleties; the thousands of sharp hairs with its millions of red shadings melding together to form a soft perfectly curved tip. He clinches the feather tight in his palm, crushing it with all his strength. He tips his head back, squeezing his eyes shut, straining to close them even tighter. He wrenches the life away from the tiny gift, a pain ringing through his loins. A tear streaks down the man's troubled face and for the first time in his life, an unknown odd feeling infects his soul: fear.

Raindrops fall one by one from the sky above.

The man opens his eyes, feeling the refreshing rain smack against his unshaven bristle-ridden face. His tear is stolen by a raindrop, dragging it down along his cheek and completely off his face.

His left hand becomes warm. The man looks down and slowly opens his clinched fingers, revealing a puddle of blood where a once thriving feather lied. The rain falls harder, causing the blood in the man's hand to quickly wash away, leaving only the fresh water from above.

The man's mouth and throat become abnormally dry, thirsting, nearly dying, for liquid. He tries to swallow, but his throat refuses. He tilts his head back once again, looking up to the sky for the water he so badly needs. But the clouds, as if reading his mind, hold their fresh water in, filling up inside, growing larger and larger. Not a drop falls, the man's serious quench for water is left unfulfilled.

An inner warmth races through his blood, traveling to each finger, every toe, and both ears as well as his nose. Numbness and tingling take over his extremities. Beads of sweat form on his forehead and his palms become sweaty. The cool crisp breeze continues to blow, but not upon the face of the disturbed man. He continues to be left vacant of relief.

His left arm becomes sore, a pain traveling from his heart, down through his shoulder, into his elbow. He loses sensation in all five of his fingers on his left hand. His chest feels as if it is about to explode, each individual breath becoming a struggle. The powerful but vulnerable man pushes himself to stand, but he lacks the strength to rise up onto his size fourteen feet. The man refuses to give an inch, as has always been the case in his life. Gritting his teeth, the simple task before him seemingly impossible, the man, the veins in his throat bulging as if they were about to burst, pushes up, not from his feet, or his knees, or his massive tree trunk thighs, but from his soul. He pushes himself and rises to his feet. But the man's tired oaks give, his body caves, and he retreats to a knee, barely keeping himself from falling back down to the ground. The pain, like an aggressive cancer spreading through its host, shoots through his left side, consuming his entire being. The man dips his head back, searching the clouds above for a single ray of light. But there is no light. There is only darkness and gloom.

"Dad! Daddy!" a voice, innocent and pure, cuts through the cold wind traveling up over the grassy Shawnee knoll. Jacob, all of nine years, comes galloping up over the swaying grass, his little legs chugging with the excitement a cool storm brings.

Jess Crestwood, the large burly man in trouble, holds strong, knowing full well his life is nearly over. He digs deep and sports a single smile for his young excitable son.

"Nature, it's everywhere, Dad!" proclaims Jacob, just now seeing the world through his own eyes for the very first time. "The lake, it's so beautiful! There are black backed ducks with yellow bills and all kinds of different colored insects," rambles Jacob energetically.

Jess does all he can to remain strong for Jacob. Without a breath in his lungs, and lacking the saliva in his mouth to swallow, he uses up nearly every bit of life remaining in his heart to shine a smile down at his boy. This shell of a giant, the ultimate pillar of broad grit and strength, rises to his feet—not grinding his teeth, or wincing in pain, not gasping for air, but simply smiling proudly over his youngest son. He looks down at his bright-eyed Jacob. "I'm proud of you, son. I'm so very proud of you," he repeats, extending his arms for a hug.

Jacob welcomes his father's loving arms, unaware of the tragedy playing out before his gentle eyes.

Jess squeezes his son, savoring every moment, knowing that at any second, it will be his last. A tear rolls down the side of Jacob's face. It's not out of fear—he remains oblivious to his father's life-threatening condition. Rather, overwhelming joy envelops Jacob's soul, responding to the tremendous love his father is bestowing upon him.

Satisfied, Jacob dashes off again. The moments slow down. Life is no longer is moving within its rules and laws. Seconds have become minutes, and with every step Jacob takes back toward Maya Lake, he realizes something is amiss. He instinctively stops, glancing back toward his father, but there is no pillar of strength. There is no broad shouldered rugged man standing tall above all other men. There is nothing but the swaying blades of the lush green Shawnee grass.

One step, then another; Jacob moves closer and closer to the spot where his father embraced him just moments before. And then he sees him. The body of his father is lying lifeless on the grass.

Jacob stares, unsure of what has become of his indestructible father. He watches in shock as the final breath empties out of his father's lungs. No words come to Jacob, only tears. The tears flow down the sides of his cheeks, but he remains still and silent. His pain and anguish are held firmly inside, relieved only by the drops of water escaping from his swelling eyes.

Thunder rolls, the crashing overwhelming Jacob's little ears. Lightning bolts fire like rockets shot out of canons across the gray sky. Torrential rain pours from the thickly bedded clouds, they themselves overcome with emotion.

Jacob tentatively steps closer to his father's lifeless body, his drenched hair and saddened face the ultimate image of loss and pain. Jacob kneels down by his father's side, his knee sinking in the soft wet grass. He remains silent, no moans or groans, but a shocking grief leaving little room for words. He lifts Jess's powerful right arm, nuzzling comfortably underneath it as he had many times before. He rests his head upon his father's still chest, curling his body up in the fetal position, resembling more a child of five, not nine. He molds to his father's being, clinching him tightly, not wanting to ever let him go.

The rain batters the two of them to no end. Jacob shuts his eyes, the tears and raindrops hardly differentiating from one another.

"I'm sorry," echoes a familiar voice. "I'm so—so sorry," the grimly apologetic voice repeats.

Ryan steps forward from a line of stray apple trees, as if he had been there all the time. It is he who is grim and apologetic. Oddly, Ryan is still twenty-six years of age, defying Father Time in this journey into the past. Nearly as curious is the displacement from reality Ryan is experiencing. As he strolls closer and closer to his father and brother, he remains dry, despite the pouring rain. Ryan drops to his knees just to the side of his dead father, sadly staring down at his younger brother cuddling up to Jess's body.

"I'm sorry," Ryan again begs for mercy from his father. "I should have been here. I should have been here."

"Yes!" Jess's disturbed voice echoes from the sky above.

Ryan snaps his head around, frightened by the heavenly presence of his deceased father.

Thunder again explodes in the sky above, matching Jess' angry voice.

Ryan stares up into the sky, which parts, the rain dissipating into nothing. He watches a ray of hope breaks through the darkness above. The sun fights its way through the blanket of gray, peeking its nose down at the world.

A hand clasps Ryan's neck, the grip strong and firm, cutting off all air to his lungs. The hand tightens, firming the grip around Ryan's neck even tighter. Ryan tries to tear the powerful hand away, but can do nothing to get air into his lungs. He tilts his head down and sees his father's dead arm extending out to his neck. Ryan's eyes bulge out in shock. Then, fear; fear from the enormous pressure being applied to his airway. Jess's eyes flare open, Ryan becoming increasingly terrified over the situation.

Jess carefully leaves a sleeping Jacob behind on the ground as he rises to his feet, standing above his eldest son, bitter and disappointed. He stares down at Ryan in disgust, a fire lit behind his glaring eyes.

"You should have been here!" The words are angrily gargled out of the intimidating monster. Rain water that has gathered in his lungs pours out of his mouth, the once mighty man resembling a possessed zombie more than a human.

"You should have been here!" The words again angrily repeated with even more vigor.

Ryan's heart drops, his fingers and toes becoming numb. The life is being squeezed completely out of his body. His eyesight blurs, the world falling out of focus. All is lost. Then…darkness.

Seven

Ryan, covered in sweat, thrusts up to a sitting position, his down comforter half off the bed. He immediately grasps at his neck, while he nearly hyperventilates to gather oxygen into his lungs. Ryan peers around his bedroom releasing short quick breaths, almost like the panting of a dog. His breathing slows, as his body calms down, returning to a more level-headed reality. Ryan takes a big relieved breath, letting out all the nervous evils from his nightmare.

Ryan is parched. His mouth is dry and his body dehydrated from his deadly adventure. He turns to his nightstand, searching for a glass of water. He raises the glass to his mouth but only a few drops of water are left. Ryan groans, reluctantly removing himself from the warm comfortable sanctity of his cotton sheets.

"Oh, man!" A rush of cold air surrounds Ryan's warm body. In just a white T-shirt and a pair of plaid boxers, Ryan tip toes out of his bedroom, briskly heading towards the kitchen.

Ryan hurriedly pitter-patters on the cold linoleum kitchen floor, wasting no time reaching for the silver hand to his Sub Zero refrigerator. Upon opening the fridge door, a light, strong and bright, surrounds Ryan's body as if he were caught directly in front of the grace of God. Almost immediately though, the light flickers, unable to maintain its overpowering brilliance. Ryan becomes annoyed by the light's erratic behavior, and flicks it with his index finger, hoping this highly professional maintenance tactic will do the trick. But the light continues to misbehave, mocking Ryan with its inconsistent flare.

Easily discouraged in his exhausted state, Ryan puts little effort into completing the task, quitting almost as abruptly as he feebly began. He grabs the carton of milk instead, pouring half a glass into the crystal held in his left hand. Ryan pushes the carton back inside, wasting no time in front of the flickering refrigerator light.

As Ryan reaches the top of the stairs, he gazes at Jacob's bedroom door, closely examining the contents taped there. He briefly reviews the Los Angeles articles, falling into a moment of reminiscence. Ryan thinks of his younger brother, concerned and confused by his entire existence. But the thought is far too big for a late night milk run.

A cool breeze nearly freezes Ryan's toes. It's cold outside and cold in the house, but Ryan is deeply confused by the existence of such a frosty breeze indoors. He moves closer to Jacob's bedroom door and holds his foot next to the bottom of the doorway. This is where the blast of cold air inside the Crestwood home is coming from. Ryan gently turns the knob of the door and shoves it open. Inside the bedroom, a cold sweeping breeze circles around Jacob's sanctuary, emanating from the open window. Jacob's pillows are missing his head, and his bedroom is missing his body.

"Jacob," Ryan grits his teeth in a frustrated, all knowing voice, confident he knows his brother's whereabouts.

Mounted on his purple and pink bike, with sparkly streamers and rainbow spokes, is Jacob. The boy is flying through the wind, his bottom lifted off his seat, riding with tremendous purpose. A rainbow ski jacket covers only half of Jacob's Batman and Robin pajamas. His hot breath is very visible in the chilled crisp air. Jacob's heart pounds, his mind starving for some peace. Jacob, his face nearly freezing, cracks a smile while staring off in the distance at his desired destination, his goal; The Shawnee Hills.

Jacob abruptly comes to a stop and looks out off the edge of the Shawnee. He looks down at Lake Maya; the crisp blue water sitting still, reflecting the light of the many stars painted in the sky above. There's a sparkle in Jacob's eyes, a settling feeling of calm and relaxation. Jacob leaves his bike and heads down the grassy hill to Maya. He runs down the side of the hill, his momentum pushing him almost uncontrollably forward.

"Ha-ha!" Jacob triumphantly shouts and laughs. He slows up just before he reaches Maya's edge, causing a flurry of fireflies to cast off into the air. Their tiny bodies glow, forming a collective shiny ball as they lift away. Jacob stares at the flying sparks in awe and excitement, like a kid in a candy shop. The air around the lake is invigorating, directly penetrating Jacob's being, sending a rush of happiness through his blood. Jacob tilts his head back gazing up at the stars. The night is clear, Mother Nature displaying her millions of wondrous night lights, each of them burning with their own individual passions. Some are small, others are larger.

Jacob removes his ski jacket, leaving just his pajamas on. Then the left shoe is flipped off, followed soon by his right. He pulls his Batman and Robin collared flannel pajama top up over his head and tosses it too on the ground. Jacob's skin clings to his bones, his frail body freezing in this cold air. But it makes no difference. He is focused, knows exactly what he's doing. Jacob removes his pants, leaving him in just his tighty-whities. Focused, the cold doesn't seem to bother Jacob. He backs up to the crest of Maya's edge, his toes just inches from her frigid belly.

Jacob closes his eyes, a grin forming on his face. He's in a strangely blissful place, spiritually in harmony with the world around. He inches out into the water, not hesitating in the slightest.

Jacob's teeth chatter, his jaw fighting the cold to remain shut and still. His eyes are deeply focused beyond the Shawnee, enveloped in a far greater purpose. The rush of ice cold water attacks Jacob's feet as he methodically backs deeper into the water. Chills are sent up the teen's legs, racing through his spine all the way to the hairs atop his head. Jacob refuses to break stride, backing even further into Maya's icy being. The water rises higher and higher on Jacob's body, his stomach and chest pulsating a thousand times a second, now his entire body shivering from the cold.

Now nearly chest high in the water, Jacob prepares himself, closing his eyes and extending his arms out like a butterfly spreading its wings. In an instant, Jacob releases all his qualms, all his worries, all his frustrations, falling straight back, cutting into the cold unkind waters of Lake Maya.

Ripples of water spread out like the shock waves of an earthquake. His body is temporarily consumed by the dark cold monster. Then…calm. The trees and flowers as well as the world surrounding the lake are silent. The world is Jacob's, the entire scene awaiting his next move.

Jacob's body surfaces, his arms and legs extended out causing him to bob up to the water's surface. Jacob has become a human raft, floating, gently, treading on Maya's skin. His eyes bolt open and an excited smile overcomes his face. The smile sends a warmth and comfort through Jacob's veins, supplying an antidote to the cold invading water. The chattering seizes, Jacob no longer affected by the icy climate. Jacob's eyes sparkle, intensely focused on the sky above.

The millions of stars in the sky are shining down upon Jacob as if he was a movie star caught in the crossfire of a spotlight. At this moment, there is no evil or hate in the world; everything is perfect. Every ball of fire is taking aim upon Jacob.

The only word for the awed feeling emanating from Jacob's soul is *wow*.

A single star strengthens, brightening in the sky, standing out from all others. Like an infection's center, the stars one by one grow brighter and stronger, rings of light forming halos around them. The stars bounce around, dancing all about the great big sky. And, slowly but surely, an object takes shape. The stars fall into a picturesque form. They become a man, a warrior of some kind, holding a colossal sword resembling the great Excalibur. The star-made swordsman performs upon the largest stage imaginable, wielding his sword around to the left, then back to the right. His technique is flawless, remaining balanced and active, displaying all the experience of a knighted warrior.

A playful *giggle* escapes Jacob's lungs, a cloud of warmth puffing out of his mouth and disintegrating into the icy atmosphere. The light show enthralls Jacob's most creative desires, his captivated eyes remaining focused on the picture show above.

Then, Jacob's attention shifts to the opposite end of the sky. There, off in the western most part of the sky, another figure is forming, similar to the zealous swordsman of the east. An adversary is born and wields his sword about, showing off his skills with the steel.

The two swordsmen recognize the other and carefully advance, taking one assured step after another. Their weapons are held high, prepared for an ensuing battle. They hold their dramatic postures, standing just yards apart, posing, and readying themselves to fight.

In the blink of an eye, they lunge forward, a spectacular clash of steel and brute strength showcased on the stage above. The light show is a fantastic feature to behold.

Jacob's mouth hangs open as his body continues to float, his pale skin featuring a touch of blue. But Jacob doesn't care about the cold, and his awe-struck face remains keyed in on the incredible images in his fantasy above.

Tick tock…tick tock…tick tock…tick tock, goes the grandfather clock. The Crestwood living room is as silent as a mouse except for the antique timekeeper.

Ryan, exhausted and frustrated, peers over at the clock, reading three on the dot. The room is dark, not a light in sight, as Ryan stews on the couch in the middle of the night. His thoughts roam: the beautiful Claire, work the next day, Jacob, and finally, the exhaustion behind his eyes. Ryan's head is slowly dropping when he hears a loud clank. The sound is consistent with someone dropping a sparkly, laced streamer bike. Ryan's head pops back up. He shakes his mind, coming to and preparing himself for the arrival of the youngest Crestwood, and the conversation that is going to follow.

With each step approaching the front door, the wood creaks more and more. And just when the creaking swells: silence.

The gold-painted front door knob slowly turns and the door is softly pushed open. A dim light from the porch temporarily shines upon Ryan's face. The door, just as softly as it was opened, is closed.

Jacob, his hair damp, short of breath, carefully slides into the dining room.

"Where have you been?" a tired and frustrated voice demands from the darkness.

Jacob jumps, caught off guard by the voice in the dark.

A lamp is switched on, shining light upon Ryan and Jacob's faces, illuminating the dining room.

The water drips down off of Jacob's wet body splashing down on the laminated wood floor below. Jacob remains still, pondering his response, while a small puddle of water forms at his feet.

"I went for a walk," says Jacob casually, as if a midnight stroll were the norm.

Ryan's eyes go to Jacob's feet, watching as small drops of water drip into a pool, intruding on his wood-finished floor. Ryan shakes his head and moves his eyes back up to his deceitful brother's face.

"Okay, so I went to the lake," Jacob gives in, recognizing he's gotten caught with his hand in the cookie jar. Jacob walks past Ryan and into the kitchen.

Ryan watches him, confused, wanting—and frankly, expecting—an excuse from Jacob. He's left alone in the living room, his arms extended out waiting, silently demanding Jacob's return.

Jacob, no mind reader, continues on his merry way into the kitchen.

Ryan throws his hands up into the air and lets out a frustrated growl, following his younger sibling into the kitchen.

"I went to the lake' really isn't good enough, Jake!" barks Ryan, visibly upset as he enters the kitchen.

Jacob, Zen-like in his state of deep calm, is standing in a pool of bright light in front of the yawning refrigerator door. The light from inside is shining absurdly brightly upon Jacob's face and body. Jacob is glowing in the wave of illumination. It is striking in the pitch-black kitchen.

Ryan looks beyond his frustration with Jacob and becomes amazed by the invigorating brilliance of the light bulb glowing from the heart of the fridge.

"I rode to the lake and went in. I know it was late, but you don't understand…you wouldn't understand why," Jacob explains, continuing to search the belly of the refrigerator with his eyes.

"Wait a second," Ryan steps forward, not caring so much about Jacob's explanation. The bright consistent fridge light has captivated Ryan's mind. Just moments before it was flickering, its life fading. Now it's shining brighter than Heaven itself. This didn't make any sense.

"That light, it was broken just an hour or so ago," Ryan, looking over Jacob's shoulder into the refrigerator, remains puzzled over the extraordinary light.

"Seems to be fine now," responds Jacob nonchalantly, grabbing the container of milk. He steps out of the bright light and moves back into the darkness to retrieve a glass for his milk.

Ryan steps into the extraordinary light, scratching his head, the fridge so bright he has trouble staring into it.

Jacob finishes pouring his glass of milk and steps in front of the enthralled Ryan. He places the milk back in the fridge and pats his older brother on the shoulder. "It's a light. Get over it," says Jacob, bluntly. He continues back over to the kitchen counter and hops up onto the tiled top, gulping down his milk.

As Ryan carefully inspects the tiny light with his eyes, the temperamental electronic device starts to flicker again, as if sensing his presence. He begins to flick the flickering light, but to no avail. The light continues to mock the frustrated Ryan. Tired of playing with it, he slams the refrigerator door shut.

"Anyway," Jacob says, continuing with his story. "I woke up and just had to leave, to ride through the cold wind and feel something…something special. So, I rode over to the lake. No biggie." Jacob takes another sip of his milk.

Ryan crosses his arms, staring at his brother, confused and annoyed. Ryan's fatherly disgust with his younger brother is boiling over.

Okay," Jacob continues, recognizing his brother's dismay. "I got to the lake and it was beautiful. The stars, the chilled air, and nature calling to me…it was all so breathtaking. I felt like I was at one with God."

"So you've found faith in the good Lord?" Ryan asks sarcastically, not buying much of Jacob's story.

"I don't know. In my own way, I felt at home. And to me, home is where your faith is. Hence, since I finally felt at home, even though I wasn't really at home, I, in a matter of speaking, may have in a very odd way, found God." The words are tossed at Ryan like a giant looping maze.

Ryan stares back at his brother with the logic still rambling through his confused head, trying to make sense of Jacob's thoughts at this late hour.

"Look. I jumped in the water, falling in back first and floated. I looked up into the stars and saw a show. It was very cool. And the show was free," Jacob smiles, hoping to lighten up the tense atmosphere.

"I don't know what you did tonight, Jake. I don't really care. All I can say is that you know better than to go ridin' off in the middle of the night. You know better than that," Ryan scolds, expressing his disappointed parental tone.

"Okay," replies Jacob simply.

"Okay…great," Ryan's disapproving sarcasm returns, and mentally throws his arms up into the air. Making little headway, and frankly, not expecting to make any at all, Ryan heads out of the kitchen and over to the staircase, just as frustrated as he was minutes before. Ryan mumbles words of confusion and disheartened, marches back up the creaky stairs.

Eight

Inside the partially built home drifts a thick layer of dust and soot. The sun pierces through some of the openings, highlighting beams of dust. The structure is slowly but surely coming together, taking the shape of a home.

Ryan is sliding his fingers along the smoothed surface of a finely sanded window sill just to the side of the front door. He's carrying out a careful inspection of the quality of his team's work.

Martin, sweat dripping down either sides of his face, comes stepping into the future kitchen sideways, with the cooler stretching out in his bulging, strong arms. He sets the cooler down in the center of the room and lets out a relieved gasp of air. He flips open the cooler, pulls out a can of beer, and closes it back up, resting his big rear on it. Martin spills a little beer and then takes a big sip, relishing the taste and moment of peace. Ryan looks at his watch and smiles, amused by his buddy's sense of time.

"It's lunch time I presume," jokes Ryan.

"Yeah, that's what my stomach's telling me."

"Break time already?" a kind and inviting voice asks from the doorway of the incomplete home. Claire has once again made an appearance at the home.

Martin respectfully hops to his feet.

Ryan takes a step toward Claire, straightening his body up as if his presiding officer just walked into the room.

"Uh…just a short one," are all the words Ryan can muster.

"Did you know he's *really* good with his hands?" Claire jokes to Martin, tossing a smile over at Ryan.

Ryan wants to hide, but has nowhere to go. He's a deer caught in headlights, taking the joke right on the chin.

"Not personally—no. But I've heard real good things," returns Martin, thoroughly enjoying his friend's uncomfortable moment.

"You boys get any work done around here with all the fun?" Claire ponders.

"Occasionally," Martin replies with a quirky smile.

"Yes…well." Claire pulls out a business card and extends her hand out to Ryan with a devious smile hiding behind her friendly grin.

Ryan takes the card, reading it with a sliver of confidence, rebounding from his most recent embarrassing moment. As he reads, his eyes widen in shock.

Martin's forehead furrows, confused, "What's it say?"

"Why didn't you tell me?" Ryan asks Claire, stupefied.

"What?" inquires Martin again.
Ryan, with a silly grin on his face, hands the card to Martin. Martin reads the card and immediately bursts into laughter. Martin, beside himself with merriment, pats Ryan on the shoulder, wishing him luck, and walks back outside. His jollity can be heard outside as Ryan struggles to find the words to respond. Claire stands before him, a cocky, playful grin on her face, shining like Polaris.

"So…you're going to be…" Ryan states, attempting to grasp the words.

"Kind of your boss," Class interrupts, happily finishing Ryan's sentence.

Ryan and Claire each look down, sharing another awkward moment.

"Hi, I'm Claire. I'm an interior designer that gets to work with a great construction crew in this beautiful small town," she reintroduces herself, extending her hand, offering to start over with a clean slate.

"I'm Ryan." The small town man gladly accepts the unknown, something he doesn't normally do. He shakes Claire's hand and the two of them share a smile not one of a casual encounter or a respectful simper, but rather a hope of a budding romance.

"It's nice to meet you," Ryan continues, well-mannered, breaking the romantic moment.

Claire lets out a gasp of laughter, amused by Ryan. "Nice to meet you, too," Claire replies kindly.

Claire and Ryan exchange a handshake, but the soft touch of their hands is no normal shake. The spark has been lit. The butterflies are chased from inside their bellies and this excitement will carry them until their next encounter.

Nine

    Jacob's body is full of sunshine as he kneels, tending to well-endowed and groomed flowers. Violets, daisies, and sunflowers, all freshly planted along the Crestwood walkway, are in full invigorating bloom. The array of vivacious colorful flowers brings life to an otherwise desolate weed-laced lawn. Jacob's attire matches the kaleidoscope of flavorful colors planted in the ground about his feet. The ensemble features a bright green pair of khaki pants and an even brighter orange long sleeve shirt. Three black lettered words have been sewn onto the orange shirt reading: I Love LA. Aqua blue socks and matching baby blue sneakers are wrapped around Jacob's suddenly flamboyant feet.

    Jacob is nothing if not unique. He tips his head back and looks up toward the sky, checking the atmosphere. A pleasant soft cool breeze makes for a refreshing late spring afternoon. A family of puffy clouds is spaced across the sky above. The sun attempts to maintain a consistent view upon the earth, but is marred by the outstretched arms of the white and gray masses above. Jacob takes in the crisp cool air, invigorated by the aura of the world, the atmosphere juicing his blood with a surge of energy. He scans around the full green oak trees. Two cardinals lift off one of the mighty oaks and gracefully glide across the partially darkened sky, adding a splash of red to the beautiful day.

    Satisfied with his secure views of the world around him, Jacob reaches inside his bright green pants's pocket and pulls out a pair of Rayban black sunglasses. Unlike most of the sunglasses Jacob's own, these happen to be *normal fitting* to the face of any human.

    Jacob hops on his blue and purple bike with sparkly streamers. Jacob shoves off down the quiet street, the sun now peeking its head through the clouds, shining upon him as he rides. Jacob is now the star of Starktown's streets, a nice spotlight shining down upon him as he makes his way down the quiet road.

Tex Potter, an eighty-five-year old Starktown lifer, is resting in his rocking chair, smoking his trusty oak pipe. His face sags from the wrinkles of time and his skin is high quality leather, most likely from the decades of pipe smoking he's participated in. A war hero from World War II, Tex has seen few things in his life that surprise him. But he sits up just a little bit more, uncharacteristically removing his trusty pipe from his lips, staring in complete bafflement at the sight before him in the street. He watches as this strange looking young man rides his streamer laced multicolored bike across his sight line.

What in the world? The question races through Tex's elderly mind, quite confused by the bizarre display before him. He continues to watch as Jacob rides off and disappears down the road. Tex rests easy back in his rocking chair returns his faithful pipe to its home, and continues to relax and puff his day away.

Jacob lifts his body up off his bike chair, riding as high into the sky as possible, the wind blasting against his inviting face. Jacob's bike races by Ma and Pa Roberts taking an afternoon stroll down the side of Cooper Street.

They watch in amazement, uncertain of their sixty-five-year old eyes.

"What's up?" Jacob greets them happily as he continues on down the road.

The elderly couple stops. They turn their heads and watch as Jacob continues to ride off.

"That boy's definitely got something wrong with him," Pa Roberts points out to his wife with a slight southern drawl.

"Amen to that, Pa," Ma agrees.

Jacob turns the corner, leaving Cooper Street behind and jets down Baker Road. Baker Road is Jacob's destination. This is where his good friend Billy lives with his grandmother.

Jacob closes his eyes, allowing the cool wind to strike against his face. He doesn't keep his eyes closed long. But he does keep them closed long enough to have a great perfect moment of peace, a moment with himself flying through the air. He can see himself as a bird soaring through the sky with limitless potential. Jacob is free, in the exact place he wants to be.

Jacob opens his eyes and rides up on the sidewalk, flying right up to the front of Billy's house.

The outside of Billy's house resembles a two-story colonial structure envious of the Deep South in the 19th century. White paint is chipping away, aged far beyond its years, leaving shards of its remains on the dirt surrounding the house. The yard has a white picket fence, if the fence can be called white anymore. The sun-stained fence looks as if it was last painted when Nixon was in office. Nearly fifty years of age has consumed the house with little more than a few touch-ups, making vain attempts at outlasting the inevitable tests of time. Rusted toys, including a tricycle and an old turquoise bike, rest on their sides on the rock hard dirt posing as a front lawn. Frost and snow have hardened the ground over the years. A deflated football, a half inflated soccer ball, and a mini basketball busting with air are spread about the dirt and weed infested so-called lawn.

Jacob wheels his clever transport over to Billy's rusty blue bike and rests it down on the ground so they're side-by-side. He skips over to the front door. A cast-iron knocker in the design of a friendly bouquet welcomes visitors. Jacob opts for the old dimly light doorbell. He pushes on the button and a muffled *ding dong* faintly circulates through the old colonial house.

The door creeks open, exposing Nana. Nana is well known in Starktown. She's survived two husbands, two heart attacks, and the deaths of two of her children. You could say that luck, or lack thereof, depending on how you look at it, finds its way to Nana in two's. Her brittle, curly gray hair rests firmly atop her head. No regular breeze is pushing Nana's cemented hair around. All of five foot three, Nana carries a hundred and seventy hefty pounds with her. Her rosy cheeks are matched only by her consistent smile, shown to all visitors upon first contact. She is a lovely woman, hard of hearing and nearing her seventy-eighth birthday. Her clothing has not been updated in nearly that long. Nana moves slowly when she has to and usually not at all. She relies on her eclectic grandson Billy for necessities.

"Hello, Jacob!" the radiant Nana welcomes.

Jacob, prepared with a big smile, in return responds plainly, "Hey, Nana." "Is it Tuesday already?" Nana inquires.

"Yep."

"Billy's in his room doin' somethin' or other. You know." Nana steps to the side, allowing Jacob to enter the house.

"Thanks, Nana," Jacob strolls by Nana into an onslaught of warm air. Nana's home is notorious for its constant summer-like temperatures, nearly matching Nana's age on any average day.

Jacob strolls up the old wooden staircase, each step creaking with pain and anguish for the footing below. The old wooden stairs are bare and old, their time long since gone. But since Nana never ventures upstairs anymore, there's no real need to replace the old flimsy steps.

Jacob moves down the dark hallway past a few old black and white pictures of Nana in her younger days. A wedding photo and a professional color picture of Nana, her two children, and her second husband, hang as a reminder of happier days. Jacob rushes right by them all, excited to enter his best friend's lair. He reaches the plain white door, the first at the top of the stairs, and carefully knocks, suspicious of what lurks on the other side.

"Come in," the soft youthful voice from deep inside the room offers.

Jacob slowly turns the knob and gently pushes the creaking door open, poking his head inside to see if it's safe.

The steel lined blinds hang low, stretching below the window sill. The blinds are only a quarter of the way open, not allowing the sun's rays to penetrate the room. Light sneaks in through the cracks, reflecting off all the lively floating lint. The day seeping in through the window is the only illumination in the mysteriously shadowed bedroom. Billy's room looks more like an experimental lab than a young man's room. Invention after invention is spread about. Toys and pieces of junk glued and tied together, creating flying and moving contraptions of all shapes and sizes, are spread about the heavily stained carpet. Tools and crafts in randomly sequenced piles are strewn next to many of the imaginative inventions.

Jacob, feeling safe, opens the door further and steps into the pseudo-laboratory.

"Hurry, close the door!" The soft voice urges.

Jacob quickly closes the door, following the voice's orders.

A strange buzzing, like that of a giant fly, bears down upon Jacob, growing louder and louder by the second.

Jacob whips his head around to find a contraption flying right at his face.

Whush! A propeller nearly nips Jacob's nose. Jacob hits the ground as if a grenade were about to go off. Like a Tonka Truck with wings multiple propellers, a rear motor, and spacious fiberglass wings allow the ground vehicle to soar around the room like a bird in flight.

"Sorry," the soft voice apologizes.

Jacob, face to the floor, looks up and sees his friend Billy, the owner of that soft, youthful voice. He's lying stomach to the ground beneath his bed, attempting to steer the flying contraption with a small remote control. A catcher's mask veils his face from sight and is accompanied by an old blue beat up chest protector. Billy looks as if he were about to receive a fastball from Nolan Ryan.

    The truck swoops and dips, nearly hitting the wall, then the floor, and on its next soar up nicks the ceiling. The plane then takes a fatal decent, smashing into the plaster chipped white wall, leaving a generous dent in its wake.

    The truck falls to pieces down on the ground.

    Feeling it's now safe in the room, Jacob and Billy hop up to their feet. Billy flips off his catcher's mask, exposing his big brown eyes and messy dirty blond hair. Billy is disappointed, slumping over the destroyed invention examining the remains of his creation.

    "Tonka Trucks," Billy begins, sadly staring down at the damaged car. "They're built damn strong, but I can't make wings strong enough to maintain its flight."

    Jacob walks up next to his good friend, towering over the much smaller sixteen-year old inventor.

    "Wanna go into the dungeon?" Billy offers to Jacob with renewed excitement, finding an immediate second wind.

    "Yeah." Jacob smiles agreeably.

    Billy's basement, and it's his, because like the upstairs portion of the house Nana doesn't travel up or down stairs due to the strenuous journey taken upon her old knees. The dungeon has become an extension of Billy and Jacob's own bedrooms and imaginations.

    The underground chamber is stacked with old toys and tools, much like Billy's bedroom. There are many books, most of which are sci-fi and fantasy that whet Jacob's deep creative appetite on the long cold winter days. The cold and dark nature of the dungeon make it inviting for spiders and other tiny crawling creatures. Spider webs hang in every corner and crevice of the cold dark room, constant reminders of who the boys share the room with.

But today the two boys are sitting side by side on old crates picking from a stack of the finest nudie magazines. From Hustler to Playboy, and even a couple of Jugs, this is a spread Heff himself would be proud of. Billy and Jacob stare in awe at the most beautiful of life's beauty, the female figure in its purest form. Their faces drop with each turn of the page, finding more amazing treasures. The two boys are nearly sweating in the seventy degree basement, their blood running warm with excitement.

"Wow," Billy mutters in awe of the centerfold he's gawking at.

"It makes you wonder why they even bother puttin' words in these things at all," Jacob says as he stares at the female anatomy.

Jacob and Billy burst into nervous laughter, and all of a sudden, there's a creak from the floorboards above. The boys freeze, holding their collective breath.

"Billy!" Nana calls from the hallway, oblivious to the current location of the boys.

Jacob shoots a concerned look over at Billy, worried Nana's on to them.

"Don't worry, she's never gonna find this place," Billy whispers with the utmost confidence. Billy sets his magazine down and hops up off his crate. "Stay here, I'll be right back."

Billy moves over to the drop ladder hanging down into the basement from the ceiling above. He reaches up, right hand first, then left, and climbs up the short ladder, gently lifting up the trap door attached to the basement ceiling.

He pushes on the trap door just a crack, making sure the coast is clear.

"Billy!" Nana calls out distantly, her voice echoing throughout the house, dulled by the many walls in between her and Billy's locale.

Confident Nana's far away, Billy stealthily slithers up into the hallway, closing the trap door, which is perfectly camouflaged by an unencumbered rug free-flowing down the entire hallway.

Claire enters what looks to be the future kitchen of the partially built two-story home. Ryan's trailing closely behind, straining to think of something to say, a peculiar cloud of guilt and embarrassment remaining over his head.

"They want solid oak cabinets, a bay window just in front of the sink over there, and don't forget to leave enough room for the Sub Zero refrigerator. The mahogany wood floors you already know about, but instead of blue and white tiles on the island and counters, we're going with a forest green and black pattern," Claire rattles off like a Sunday grocery list.

Ryan's still deep in his own mind, guilt of uncomfortable proportions infecting his every thought, urging, almost begging him to cleanse his soul. "Ya know, when I said I was good with my hands, I really meant construction and stuff-I'd never-ya know…"

Ryan's interrupted by a soft pleasant finger strategically placed over his lips. Claire steps forward, her index finger resting against Ryan's mouth, his breath quickening, his heart beat elevating. His sincere speech has come to an abrupt end, but he has little to complain about.

"First things first. Nod if you understand what I told you about the kitchen?"

Ryan nods, very agreeable with the angelic beauty who's now leading this small town native by the nose.

"Good. I'll pick you up at six thirty tonight." Claire declares assertively.

Claire awaits a response from Ryan, tilting her chin down, her eyes widening. He quickly obliges with repeated short, quick nods.

"You're going to give me your card with your home phone number and address on it," Claire slowly and carefully explains to Ryan, as if he were an eight-year old.

Ryan nods again.

"Good." Claire removes her finger from Ryan's mouth and gracefully glides away from the stunned and speechless man. She stops underneath the door frame and pirouettes back to Ryan. "Oh, and you shouldn't apologize about being good with your hands." One last smile and then Claire flees, leaving Ryan yet again stunned by the dizzying conversation.

Martin re-enters the kitchen, strutting into the room with a ham sandwich stuffed in his mouth. Ryan's mouth is hanging open, his eye widened and fixed on nothing in particular. His mind wanders, captured under Claire's magical spell.

"Hey, baby, you get the phone number of that mac truck that just ran you over?" Martin jokingly asks.

"You wouldn't believe me if I told you," Ryan responds, remaining awestruck.

Martin smiles and nods, letting out a friendly chuckle. He stuffs his face with another giant bite of his sandwich.

A thought hits Ryan and he frantically searches his pockets for a business card. He comes up empty and turns to Martin. "You wouldn't happen to have a business card on you?"

Martin shakes his head and chuckles once again, thoroughly amused by his best friend. Martin exits the kitchen, leaving Ryan all alone.

Ten

At twelve stores tall, Starktown's Medical and Care Center is the tallest building in town. Fire red bricks make up the foundation of the giant structure. Many windows, highlighted indentions in the brick walls, mark the sides of medical center. On the eighth floor steel wires intertwine with one another, crossing and weaving from one end of the frame to the other. The restrained eighth floor windows make the rooms inescapable. Hospital, care home, and psychiatric ward: the building provides care for a whole array of people and their health issues. Jacob and Billy come charging up over Broward Corner and, cross over Broward Bridge, a tiny wooden connection which stretches all of twenty feet across two soft marshy grass plains, which used to hold a small river that shared the same name.

Broward Road stretches three miles, most of them leading to Starktown's Medical Center.

Jacob and Billy are laughing along, the two teenagers racing down the dirt road, quickly approaching the hospital. Jacob leads by just one bike length, but it's a small lead, one that Jacob controls with each turn of his sprockets. The smaller, struggling legs of Billy churn wildly to keep up with the coasting Jacob, as the two do every Tuesday afternoon.

Jacob just ekes out Billy as the two come to a fantastic screeching halt in front of a corroded bike rack. They are winded, breathing heavily, both smiling. Jacob unlocks a chain wrapped tightly around his bike's neck. Billy watches as Jacob secures their bikes together.

The two boys enter the quiet care center, their smiles fleeing away. The cold floors and off-white walls, the cultivation of supreme plainness, bring about feelings of loneliness and vulnerability that consumes both boys' heads. No talking, no joking around. They walk by a nurse wheeling a food cart, neither boy making eye contact with her. They keep their heads down, walking shoulder to shoulder, sticking close together. They approach an elevator, both boys remaining silent. Jacob turns to his younger, more intimidated friend.

"It'll all be okay," Jacob reminds him, attempting to soothe Billy's nerves.

Billy projects a nervous smile and bobs his head up and down two brief times.

They enter the steel door elevator. Jacob pushes the button for floor eight. The button lights up and the steel doors shut, leaving the two boys in the extra-large space, used mainly to transport patients up and down the floors of the hospital.

The *therapy room* as it's called, is the first room they see when the cold steel doors of the elevator tremble open. Jacob and Billy hesitantly and quietly approach the door, walking on egg shells so as to not alert anyone to their presence. The room is fairly spacious, allowing for many more than just the three loonies and the one and only psychiatrist.

"Hey, boys, come and have a seat," Doctor Wells tells the boys placidly, expecting their shy entrance.

Billy and Jacob sneak into the room, all eyes turning towards them. The other three sets of eyes are also teenagers. Their looks are each very distinct. Cara is by far the best looking of the bunch. Her eyes are blackened by a combination of a lack of sleep and cosmetic touch-ups. She wears black eyeliner running from the corner of her eyes to the sides of her head. Her all-black clothing caps off her dramatic *goth* appearance. Her skin is pale, her eyes blue. Despite being a beautiful day, the black trench coat she wears further draws attention to her appearance. Although she is dressed like darkness, Cara has a sweetness struggling to get out. Maybe it was the abuse of her step-father before they hauled him off to jail, or the fact that she suffers from certain aspects of OCD, but clearly there is much more to

Cara than meets the eye. With her head tilted down, her eyes carefully peer out of her darkness to catch a glimpse of Billy. Billy intrigues Cara, both haunted by quiet chaotic pasts that haunt their minds, both with overwhelming secrets a child should never be burdened with. Billy, of course, is oblivious to her attention.

Vinni Casterelli—the name alone strikes fear into the hearts of any and all teenagers in Starktown. The tough little Italian hoodlum, his baggy pants sagging low as to show off the boxers of the day, his finely combed slicked back hair, his broad shoulders, arrogant strides, and throwback nineteen-fifty's T-shirt, encapsulates all that the eighteen year old Casterelli is about. Whereas Vinni is stocky and a little bit short, his thug twin and best friend, Casey Howard, is tall and thin. Casey, nearly six feet three inches tall, dressed in a black Chicago White Sox jersey, a matching black Sox hat worn backwards, two gold chains hanging around his neck, and a tall slim frame, thinks of himself as a boy from the ghettos of New York. In actuality, he's never been out of Starktown. Casey is a bully and an all-around bad seed, no rhyme or reason for his violent tendencies. Vinni, on the other hand, has all the alcoholic abusive father reasons in the world to be mean. The two boys are a tandem of evil for young teens in this small town. They are the top of the food chain and quite often feed on those who reside below them.

"I wanna leave," blurts out Vinni impulsively as Jacob and Billy take their seats.

Vinni and Casey shoot Jacob an evil look. It's the kind of look you deliver to your mortal enemy. Meanwhile, Jacob just smirks at the two boys as if knowing something they could never understand. Billy looks away, his eyes doing everything to avert looking Vinni and Casey directly in the eyes.

"We calling it, already?" Jacob asks hopefully, knowing full well Doctor Wells is nowhere near ending the session.

"No, Jacob," replies Doctor Wells calmly. He then turns to Vinni. "Just a few minutes more Vinni. We haven't had a chance to talk yet."

Vinni is not thrilled about being there and settles for crossing his arms and a small huff to further get his point across.

Casey chimes in with, "He started the fight!" Casey's finger is pointed sharply at Vinni. "I didn't do it. I don't know why I have to be here." Casey plays innocent victim.

"Did not!" Vinni replies.

"Did so," Casey digs again.

"They deserved it," Vinni finds a middle ground with his best friend.

"True. They definitely did!" Casey agrees, and the two boys laugh over their mutually chaotic behavior.

"Boys. That's not okay," Doctor Wells chimes in with a disapproving tone and glare.

"Yeah-yeah. We know," Vinni concedes.

"But it was fun," Casey jokes under his breath, drawing another smile from his best bud.

Doctor Wells stares at the two boys with some frustration. His anger is well-intended and the boys adjust their attitudes and themselves in their seats, sitting up straight and sporting apologetic facial responses.

"Sorry, Doc," they apologize in unison.

Doctor Wells excuses their misguided comments but knows there is a lot of work to be done with those two boys.

Cara very subtly lifts her tucked chin up and grabs a glance of Billy. He is currently whispering to Jacob, the two of them engaged in their own private conversation. Cara smiles—not a normal smile, a sacred smile. She sees something in Billy that brings the best out of her, something she struggles with on her own. Although he has no idea, her star-crossed look speaks a thousand positive words over the three seconds she grabs a stare.

When Jacob turns back towards Vinni and Casey, Cara once again buries her chin down, her eyes following, the quiet girl going back into her shell.

"Let's all keep things positive," Doctor Wells interjects. "Jacob, Billy, you guys came in a few minutes late, but Vinni and Casey were having some issues outside of the realm of acceptable, using violence to solve their problems."

"Again?" Jacob asks nonchalantly.
"Jacob," Doctor Wells uses a stern tone with Jacob, insinuating the young man knows better than to incite the other two youngsters.

Vinni mouths, *"You're dead"*, to Jacob.
Jacob winks back at Vinni, making the young Italian hothead none-too-happy.

"Why don't you boys add something today?" Doctor Wells poses, opening the door for Jacob and Billy to participate, sharing some of their own issues.

Billy leans over and whispers in Jacob's ear, the two conferring as if they were sharing one voice. And that voice, of course, is Jacob's.

"I, me speaking for Billy of course," Jacob begins. "think that I want to be an inventor. I want to create new planes—planes that can fly as fast as sound can travel." Jacob turns to Billy. "That's very cool by the way." Billy smiles, happy Jacob approves.

Vinni rolls his eyes, annoyed to even be present during this discussion.

"What brought on this sudden surge of creative energy?" Doctor Wells poses, with a playful intrigued smile. Billy leans over to again speak to Jacob, this time a little concerned by the snooping question.

"Come on," Vinni crows, annoyed.

"Easy, Vin," Doctor Wells again shoots Vinni a look and holds out his hand, preaching patience with his eyes.

Jacob holds his hand up, reassuring Billy he has things under control.

"It's kind of a secret. You know, covert. So if we told you, we'd have to probably kill you. And then we wouldn't be able to come here on Tuesdays any more. That would kinda suck."

"I'm gonna kill somethin'," Casey adds, under his breath.

Doctor Wells smiles, trying to hold in his laughter, amused by Jacob and Billy and oblivious to Casey's rude comment. "Okay." Doctor Wells gives in, not prying a second longer. "Billy, have you thought about enrolling in art classes. Cara just enrolled in a new art class."

"I actually just dropped out," Cara says quietly.

"Really? Why?" Doctor Wells asks with concern.

Billy's quiet eyes flash up towards Cara, her response piquing his interest. His curiosity about her mirrors her own about him. They have a silent cat and mouse game being played out with their kind eyes.

"I just…" Cara feels everyone's eyes bearing down upon her and immediately regrets chiming in. "Just…forget it." Cara tries to shut down the conversation.

"When you feel up to it, Cara," Doctor Wells eases the young teen down and gives her the out she needed.

Billy's eyes flash down and away, sensing the conversation being moved back in his direction. "Well, Billy. Back to you. Art classes?" Doctor Wells gets back on track.

Billy leans over to Jacob to communicate his response. Before he can complete his thought, Doctor Wells interrupts.

"No, Billy, *you* answer me. Tell me…in your own words."

76

Billy shrugs, not wanting to speak aloud. He looks around at all the curious faces bearing down on him, and that stirs his nerves, making him even more apprehensive to speak.

"Art classes could be great. Or you can try and look into trade schools for inventing for the future?" Doctor Wells barrages Billy with ideas, desperately hoping he'll bite on one.

Billy shrugs once again, giving little clue about any of his desires.

"Okay, you think about it again this week. We'll get back to it next time." Doctor Wells lets Billy off the hook, backing off his questions, and offering simply his support.

Therapy lasts about another thirty minutes, the kids not as forthcoming as the good doctor would hope.

"All right. You all are excused," Doctor Wells dismisses the kids as if they were back in school.

Vinni and Casey angrily glare at Jacob and Billy as they get up. Billy again averts his eyes in any other direction.

Jacob just smiles at them, showing no signs of fear on the outside, but on the inside, he is terrified.

"We're outta here," Vinni and Casey exit the room showing no growth as they wear their anger on their sleeves.

Cara slips out right behind them, saying little as she sneaks away.

Billy gets up and exits the room and then bobs his head back into the room.

"I'll be with Crazy Eddie," Billy says, and he disappears, closing the door behind him.

Jacob is sitting in a chair in the therapy room, the only teen left.

Doctor Wells finishes writing some notes down on a yellow pad. Wells smiles and sits back in his chair.

"Billy likes water fountains," Jacob says, feeling a little uncomfortable with the one on one session.

"Yes. He does. He likes watching the running water. Why do you think?"

"It calms him," Jacob confidently replies.

"I think so too. I want you to keep on encouraging Billy to speak for himself. It's very important for him to come out of his shell." "Okay."

"How are you doing, Jacob? How has life been?" Doctor Wells turns his attention back to Jacob.

"Fine."

"Taking your medicine and still going fishing down at Lake Maya?" Doctor Wells asks, in a more amiable approach.

"Yeah," Jacob answers, his demeanor and body language distant and removed from the conversation.

Doctor Wells immediately recognizes Jacob's attention deficit. "I'd like to get together with you alone sometime in my office. We can talk about anything—your brother, your mom, your dad. Whatever you'd like."

"Ryan's fine…dad's dead, mom's nuts." Jacob is blunt yet placid in his response.

"I know, Jake," Doctor Wells says solemnly. "I have some time tomorrow, right about noon time. You think you can come down here at noon tomorrow? And we'll just talk a little while, whatever's on your mind."

"Okay."

"You gonna go visit with your mother today?"

"Yeah. Billy went to see his uncle, so, I might as well," Jacob halfheartedly responds.

"Okay. You go wish her well for me. I'll see you tomorrow."

Jacob turns and heads towards the door. He stops, a thought striking him as odd. He turns back to the good doctor.

"You know Doc…" Jacob begins, grabbing the full attention of Doctor Wells, more than happy to listen to what his young patient has to say. "Parents tell you as a child not to talk to strangers. It was one of the last things Billy's mom told him before she made herself dead. He saw her put that gun in her mouth."

"Yes, I remember," a simple melancholy response. "You always keep a good eye on Billy, but especially take care of yourself. Okay?" Doctor Wells requests warmly.

"Sure thing, Doc." Jacob turns and exits the therapy room, leaving the door open behind him.

Doctor Wells is left gazing in Jacob's wake, deeply concerned about this young man's mental state.

The halls of the psychiatric ward are pure white, as if recently painted. The brightness of the walls are complemented by the bright white lights shining from behind plastic barriers above. The hallway is quiet, most of the doors shut. There is an eerie silence in the ward, a sense of solitude for those who live within their own thoughts.

However, there is one door at the end of the hall cracked a few inches open. Natural light seeps into the restrictive white hospital lighting, adding a touch of realism in an otherwise very cold, removed place.

Jacob approaches that one open door and slowly slips inside, quietly pushing the door back to a mere crack opening.

The room is warm. Light is penetrating through the window, whose blinds have been pulled completely up. Sitting in her old torn up teal recliner is Doris Crestwood. Doris's gray streaked hair is thin and brittle, hanging down just below her shoulders. She turns, exposing only the right side of her shadowed face. At first Doris grins devilishly, her eyes squinting, her face worn and wrinkled. Her grin fades into a deceptive smirk, the mysteries and secrets of the world hiding behind her cloudy, desolate gray eyes. The deceitful glow lasts but a second, and then Doris turns her attention back to the outside world, which lies far beyond that of her own.

"Hey, mom." Jacob's greeting falls on deaf ears. "Mom?"

"I'm just watching Agnes walk up the stairs. I'll give you three to one on her making it up without falling," Doris states, firmly focused on her old friend Agnes as she methodically moves up a set of stairs down below. Doris' voice is thick, scruffy, and deep. She puts a sinister drag on each letter muttered, as if there were an evil plan behind each one of her thoughts. She is blunt and direct, knowing little in the way of compassion and love. These words are no longer a part of her life.

"No thanks." Jacob has little interest in the fine art of gambling.

Doris stares anxiously, her left foot tapping on the floor. She winces, her body language pulling back, her teeth gritting. She takes a deep breath, holding it for a moment and then lets out a frustrated and angry sigh.

A grumble of frustration erupts from inside the belly of the elder Crestwood. Doris spins her recliner around, facing Jacob. "The old hag got lucky. You should have made the bet," Doris insists as if Jacob had lost something by not betting.

"Maybe next time, mom. Maybe next time."

"Yeah. Anyway." Doris forgets the whole Agnes incident and moves on with her thoughts. "So…how'd we do in the game last night?" Doris rubs her hands together, earnestly awaiting her son's response.

Jacob walks over to his mother's bed and tosses down a small wad of money wrapped in a rubber band with an accompanying deck of cards. "We did well." Jacob displays a victorious confident grin, similar to his mother's.

Doris's smile widens, her eyes sparkling with pride. "What'd I tell you? We couldn't lose with my lucky deck."

"You mean marked deck."

"Hey, you'd be surprised, I've made a pretty penny in Gin-Rummy since I've been cooped up in this palace," says Doris, making a defensive stand.

Jacob smiles as they both fall uncomfortably silent, their conversation having run its course. Moments pass by with each of them unsure of what to say next.

"So, you wanna play?" Doris hints at a friendly card game with her son, showcasing her devious pearly whites.

"What?" Jacob is caught a little off guard.

"Say…five card draw? Buck a hand?" Doris shuffles the cards, snapping the cards around her hands quicker than the eye can focus.

"Sure," Jacob agrees suspiciously.

Doris is set to deal out the cards when Jacob holds up his hand, stopping her.

"No-no. Not with that deck. It's the marked one, remember?"

"You're learnin'!" Doris, smiles, proud of her son. Doris reaches into the top drawer of a small nightstand and pulls out a fresh deck of cards. Again she shuffles like a Vegas dealer, perfectly slinging the cards out, one for Jacob, one for her, until five cards rest in each of their piles.

They each pick up their personal stack of cards, closely examining the hand they've been dealt. Jacob arranges his, deep in thought, attempting to calculate his next move. Doris, meanwhile, is peering over the tops of her cards with an evil, chilling grin, knowing more than just the straight up hand is before the two of them.

"How many ya want?" Doris waits intensely for a response from Jacob, a snake poised to make a kill.

Jacob struggles with his thoughts for a moment. Reluctantly, he tosses three cards down. "Give me three."

Doris tosses him three cards. Shortly after, she tosses just one down into the pot. "I'll take just one," her confident and cocky glow seems more like the expression of an arch villain than a poker player. "Whatcha got?" Doris again anxiously presses Jacob.

"Two pair." A nonchalant and hopeful Jacob lays down a pair of sevens and eights.

Doris maintains her treacherously optimistic glare. She casually lays down her five cards, displaying them like a string of pearls. All five cards are aces, the first and last both spades.

Jacob stares at the cards with a whirl of confusion racing through his head. "Five aces?" he asks. "I didn't know it was possible to get five aces," Jacob naively inquires.

"Of course it's possible!" Doris replies without hesitation. "Don't you see I got five of 'em showing?"

"Cool!" Jacob excitedly blurts out. "I've never seen that before!"

"It's pretty rare." Doris surveys the situation, checking to see if Jacob is on to her con. But he's none the wiser, staring at the amazing, superhuman five ace hand. "Wanna play again?"

"Sure." Jacob, much like an oblivious child, jumps at the losing proposition.

Doris again shuffles the cards and deals them out. "You owe me a buck…workin' on two." Doris's sinister grin is now more prevalent than before.

Eleven

Tuesday night is a kind of ritual around the Crestwood household; the only thing the two brother's share with one another.

Jacob is scurrying about the kitchen dressed in a classic puffy white chef's hat, with an accompanying *Kiss the Cook* apron. His hands, apron, and even his right cheek are all stained with chunky tomato sauce. The invigorating aromatic blend of Parmesan and garlic tantalize the nostrils, as the scent sweeps through the house like a strengthening storm.

Jacob sprinkles the last dashes of Parmesan over a grand presentation of four chicken breasts with shredded mozzarella and Ragu blanketing the skinless meat. Jacob lets out a sigh and ogles over his superb creation.

"Fantastico!" Jacob blows a kiss at his masterpiece, taking on the persona of a fine Italian chef.

Ryan comes strutting into the kitchen, grinning absurdly, excited about his forthcoming date. A white turtleneck peeks out from under a dark blue sweater. Black khaki pants draws attention down to fine black Gucci dress shoes, freshly shined for an evening out.

"Smells good," Ryan comments.

Jacob turns and looks Ryan over, perplexed by the extravagant levels he's gone to for a Tuesday night dinner.

"Nice digs. You didn't have to get all dressed up for me though," Jacob responds, sensing something may be amiss. Jacob notices his father's Gucci shoes freshly shined on Ryan's feet. He knows something's up.

"I thought I told you," Ryan tries to play Jacob, already diving headfirst into his excuse. "I'm going out with an old buddy of mine."

"Going out? It's Tuesday night. I make dinner on Tuesday nights," Jacob rambles.

"I'm sorry. This friend of mine, he's coming all the way down here just to see me. He's an old friend. He's come a long way." Ryan digs himself deeper and deeper into his trench.

"Coming down?" Jacob suspiciously begins his interrogation, knowing full well something's rotten in the state of Denmark.

"Yeah…you know…from up north," Ryan points up towards the ceiling, stuttering along, ill prepared to answer Jacob's cross-examination. Ryan turns red with a nervous smile, realizing he's pointing up towards God, not north.

Ryan re-points his finger in the correct direction.

Jacob flashes his disapproving eyes up at the ceiling where Ryan was pointing just moments ago, and like an animal sensing a weakness in his prey, he attacks. "Where abouts up north?"

"You know…umm…umm…Canada. My Canadian friend from up north is finally visiting me." Ryan, shaky at best, asserts with wondering eyes his outlandish fabrication.

"Canada," Jacob says to himself.

Ryan holds his breath, hoping, praying for Jacob to buy his apprentice-like lie.

"Okay," Jacob responds, appearing to let Ryan off the hook. He casually turns his attentions back to his award winning meal. He opens up the preheated oven and carefully slides his tray of well-prepared Italian cuisine inside.

"Aren't you upset?" Ryan asks curiously, feeling the guilt already sinking in from his deception.

"Upset? Me? Why?" Jacob wipes down the counter, going on with his business as if the disappointing conversation with his older brother never occurred.

"Okay…good." Ryan lets out a tiny breath of air he had held inside, somewhat relieved he fooled Jake. He turns and slowly vacates the kitchen, thinking about his planned escape soon to come.

"Have fun," Jacob adds, knowing full well the battle for the evening has only just begun.

Jacob's bedroom is lit by his computer monitor. Jacob, a great swordsman, is battling a dragon on his way to securing the safety of the damsel in distress. He pauses, sensing something. The slamming of a car door confirms Jacob's suspicions.

Just outside the Crestwood house, a pair of beautiful feet, dressed in black high-heeled sandals, swagger down the walkway up to the front door.

The doorbell alerts the rest of the house that company has arrived.

Ryan is impatiently seated on the couch, eagerly tapping his feet. Upon hearing the presence of a visitor he springs up to his feet, rushing over to the door. He lunges for the doorknob, then stops, glancing back at the staircase, checking to see if the coast is clear. He's relieved; no sight of Jacob. He opens up the door and finds a vibrant, breathtaking Claire. Her smile immediately lights up Ryan's dull world. A ray of possibilities shines on Ryan, his mouth breaking upwards, returning Claire's smile with one of his own. Claire's maroon silk blouse is tucked firmly inside an elegant ankle length black skirt. Pearls decorate her neck and ears and she wears a sensual red on her lips. The moment is perfect.

"You look beautiful," Ryan utters in awe of his beautiful date.

"Thank you," Claire gratefully smiles. "And you look good, too."

"Thanks," Ryan blushes in response.

Claire looks over Ryan's shoulder, showing a tiny inkling of entering the warm home.

Ryan regains his senses, stepping out of Claire's spell, realizing a strange younger brother could be looming over his shoulder. He steps in front of Claire's view, filling the doorway like a wall.

"Aren't you gonna invite me in?" Claire asks with a confused, somewhat amused smile.

"Um…," Ryan repeatedly glances back, now growing more and more nervous.

"Just for a minute," Claire begs kindly. "I want to see your house. It says a lot about a person."

That's what I'm afraid of, Ryan thinks, knowing full well his home is full of many voices that may be heard.

Ryan nods and smiles, ultimately giving in to Claire's charm. He steps to the side, silently conceding entrance into the house.

Claire strolls inside, passing by the now much more nervous Ryan. Claire leaves a calming scent of beauty in her wake, the kind of special lotions and sprays kept in women's bathrooms. Ryan takes a deep breath, making a last second wish for peace and serenity, as he closes the front door, enclosing the two of them inside.

In Jacob's bedroom his computer remains on, a screen saver of dragons, red and black, flying back and forth across the screen in the background of a dark, gray sky. Some are closer than others and appear quite large, while others are far away, and small. There are many dragons in the bedroom, but no signs of a bright-eyed dirty blond hair boy. Jacob has left the room.

Back in the living room, Claire is deliberately strolling through, paying close attention to each and every dusty, ancient trinket scattered about. Pictures set in old frames, haunting reminders of the past, the grandfather clock which stands prominently in the room are all clues to who the Crestwood's were. The thick layers of dust time has embedded in many of the fine creations leads Claire on a train of interesting thoughts. The positions of the items have seemingly been the same for years. How many? Who knows? The wall patterns and positioning of the many antiquities and homely items scream outdated. The room is more indicative of nineteenth century Europe, maybe Great Britain—not Starktown, Illinois. Claire is fascinated by the virtual museum she sees before her. Everything in the room belongs together—everything except the people that live in it.

"I like it. It's…cozy," Claire says, still intrigued with the room around her.

"It's home," Ryan adds, more worried about Jacob making a cameo.

Claire spots the finely crafted chessboard. "Oh! I love chess." She turns back to Ryan but her eyes fade over his left shoulder. Claire sports a suspiciously silly smile.

Ryan snaps his head around to see what Claire's looking at, the worst of his fears realized. Standing at the entrance to the living room, with his chest thrust forward like a hero standing tall, is Jacob. He's dressed in his puffy chef's hat and matching outfit.

"Wow, Rye. Your guy friends are getting a heck of a lot better lookin'!" Jacob points out sarcastically. The battle has begun.

"Claire, this is my brother, Jacob." Ryan, concedes his younger sibling's existence, all the while trying to refrain from a developing scene.

"Hello, Jacob," Claire says, with a kind and inviting smile.

Jacob slowly approaches Claire, staring at her intensely. He appears possessed. He's a confident man in the body of a young boy approaching this elegant beauty. A visible contradiction, Jacob removes his hat with his right hand and reaches out with his left, taking her soft right fingers in his own. He leans down, smoothly kissing the back of her fragile, soft hand.

"It's a pleasure to meet you…Claire. Just Claire?" Jacob, the great Casanova, asks.

"Just Claire," she states with a mild amusement, but a subtle giggle follows. On a subconscious level, Claire has been charmed by the younger, unusually engaging, *Don Juan* Crestwood.

"Just Claire it is." Jacob steps back from his romantic interlude.

Ryan is standing off to the side in shock. He has never in his life seen his brother talk to a girl for any extensive period of time, let alone become a romantic poet. Ryan steps in front of Jacob's new prize and draws Claire's sweet eyes to his own.

"Are you ready to leave?" Ryan asks Claire, still taken with her beauty, but now desperate to flee his brother's embarrassing grasp.

Jacob peeks his head out from behind the taller and more masculine Ryan. "That's a magnificent dress," Jacob compliments, also desperate for the attention of this beauty.

"Thank you." Claire grins and nods to Jacob, flattered and happily accepting his compliment.

"Yeah, it sure is," Ryan lags behind his younger brother, now falling victim to the war being waged.

"Ya know, I used to have one just like it," Jacob jokes.

Claire laughs alone with Jacob. Ryan, feeling left out, reluctantly chuckles, feeling the moment has slipped away from his control.

"You guys going to dinner now?" Jacob asks.

"Yep," Ryan replies abruptly, the anger and frustration in his belly now growing with every moment spent in his younger brother's presence.

"Why waste your time? Stay here and eat."

"Stay here?" Claire asks curiously, anticipating an extraordinary response from the young witty teen.

"Think of it like this," Jacob begins. "You're going to spend at least forty-five minutes round-trip in driving alone. Then, once you finally arrive at the restaurant, you'll have to wait at least ten minutes more to get a table. You have to read a menu with the tiniest print, pay too much money for at best, average food, and the final insult is tap water with a lemon to conceal all the toxins in the contaminated liquid. And on top of all of that, you have to wait at least thirty minutes for your under cooked, luke-warm food. Now, I'm no mathematician, but that's a lot of minutes to waste that you'll never get back in your life. Before you know it, you'll be fifty and you will have spent one-fifth of your life driving and waiting just to eat food, when all the while, it was right in front of your nose. If you ask me, that's a big bummer."

Claire smiles, amused and impressed by Jacob's magnetic presentation.

"Sometimes people like to take their time and wait," Ryan chimes in, rather weakly returning fire after Jacob's barrage of verbal missiles.

"Ya know, Ryan, in a weird way, your brother has a good point," Claire adds, seemingly weighing in on Jacob's behalf.

Jacob turns to Ryan, his arms crossed, a victorious smile on his face.

"He does?" Ryan asks Claire, almost shocked over her alliance with Jacob.

"So, what does the great chef have on tap for dinner?" Claire submits to Jacob, tossing the ball back into his court.

Jacob perks up, pleasantly surprised by the question posed to him. "The main entrée is chicken parmigiana and it will merely cost you your presence and pleasant company."

"Sounds like a bargain," responds Claire, playing along with the young teenager. "Cool," Jacob responds happily. Claire walks off into the kitchen.

Jacob continues to smile, ecstatic over the night's recent developments. Jacob tries to hold in his excitement, decisively defeating his brother in the first battle of the evening.

Ryan, the elder statesmen of the family, shakes his head, disagreeing with the path Jacob has chosen for the evening. "What's the matter with you? What are you thinking?" Ryan attacks, with the fury of a father, not a brother.

"Whatcha talkin' about?" Jacob answers, playing dumb.

"Boy, this smells great!" Claire comments from inside the kitchen.

Jacob pivots to Ryan, again displaying the same triumphant smile as exhibited earlier. Jacob trots towards the kitchen, leaving a disbelieved Ryan in his wake. Ryan, alone in the living room, is frustrated and aggravated.

"Jacob," Ryan grumbles under his frustrated breath. He reluctantly follows Jacob and Claire into the adjoining room.

The dining room table is decorated with two burning candles in rusty silver holders. An antique silver tray provides the centerpiece on a fine, old cotton tablecloth. The tray is holding the well-displayed chicken parmigiana, under a thin layer of cheese and marinated perfectly in a sea of Ragu. Three empty holes have been left by meat which has made its way to the patrons' and chef's plates. Set next to the shiny silver antique tray is a large wood kneaded basket filled with a half-dozen buttery Hawaiian rolls.

Jacob and Claire finish up, each of their plates are virtually cleaned to the point of seeing their own reflections.

Ryan's platter is nearly untouched. The elder Crestwood remains bitter, almost bored by the meal at home.

"That was delicious!" comments Claire as she wipes her face clean. "Where did you learn to cook like this?" She asks Jacob with intrigue.

"Food and Cooking channels," responds Jacob as if it were a no-brainer. "I learn a new dish each week." Claire chuckles at first, waiting for some kind of punch-line, believing Jacob is pulling her leg.

Jacob sports a sincere expression from his side of the table, showing little sign of joking around.

Claire's chuckles immediately fade, her mindset changing one-hundred and eighty degrees. "Really?" Now a more impressed Claire heads on an information gathering expedition.

"Yeah, it's easy," Jacob responds, happily and nonchalantly.

Ryan pays little attention to the conversation, removed from the reality before him. Never in his wildest dreams did Ryan think he'd be playing the co-starring role he's been cast to play thus far in the evening.

Claire's smile sparks excitement and warmth in Jacob's belly. He tilts his head, staring at the beautiful woman. The suave Don Juan all of a sudden morphs back into an intimidated sixteen year old boy. Jacob, for the first time in the evening, is silenced. He turns back to his plate and everyone finishes up dinner.

Ryan briskly leads Claire to the front door, not wanting Jacob to toss any more wrenches into his evening plans.

"Oh, hey, you guys leaving so soon?" asks Jacob, as he rushes in from the other room, for the first time desperate and concerned. His focus has completely shifted away from Ryan and is now bent on keeping the lovely angelic breath of fresh air in his sight.

"We've gotta catch a movie," Claire says regretfully, enjoying the quaint Crestwood family dinner.

"Yeah, we're gonna get there a little early so we can *wait* in line," Ryan sarcastically adds.

"Are you sure? 'Cause we could stay here and have a round-robin chess tournament," Jacob offers.

"You don't even know how to play chess," Ryan strikes back, now playing the starring role of big brother.

"Overconfidence is your weakness," Jacob returns with all seriousness, desperation taking over. He's thrown down a gauntlet, optimistic his challenge to an old western duel could keep Claire in the home for at least an hour longer.

"Good night, Jacob," Ryan states in finality, ignoring Jacob's sarcasm and dousing all attempts by his younger brother to keep them detained. Ryan turns his attention back to Claire, hoping a smile and opening the front door will lead her outside. The quicker he moves, the less likely Jacob will pique Claire's interest and, once again, squash another part of the evening's activities.

"It was a pleasure meeting you, Jacob."
Jacob gasps, inevitable defeat intensifying inside his head. "Likewise…Just Claire."

"Dinner was great, little brother." Ryan senses victory at hand.

Ryan's kind, if belittling, words fall on deaf ears. An entranced Jacob watches as an angel dashes out of his helpless grasp. Butterflies dancing in his stomach slow, electric tingling at the tips of his fingers and toes subside, and his mood swings south as the front door closes behind the budding couple.

"Just Claire," Jacob silently mumbles to himself, continuing to stare at the bare front door, a cold blast of air from outside momentarily smacking his warm face.

The streets are damp outside, a light icing of dew canvassing all of Starktown. A slow moving fog is rising off the cold cement streets, the brisk post-winter air taking hold of the small town.

Ryan and Claire exit the local movie theater, both blasted with the overwhelming prospect of a chilly night out.

"Brr," they both agree, immediately bringing their hands to their mouths, blowing as much warmth inside their cupped fingers as possible.

"Oh, my gosh, it's so cold!" Claire exclaims, rushing her wool-knit jacket over her shoulders. Ryan, the gentleman that he is, quickly comes to her aid, helping her get the jacket on.

The new couple walks side by side, their arms hanging down beside one another. Ryan takes the initiative, gently taking Claire's hand in his own. They continue on, their relationship gaining momentum by the second.

"So, in your opinion Miss Claire," Ryan begins, like a legal eagle debating before the highest court in the land. "Do you believe you have at all wasted your life by traveling and waiting to see this fine cinematic presentation with me? Or, was your time well spent? Of course, you did have the luxury of my company all evening." Ryan says with a sarcastic smile, now more comfortable with this mysterious angelic creature.

"I think I'll go with the second one for now," Claire smirks, playfully responding to Ryan. Their moonlight walk continues, and although it's quite cold, their hearts remain warm.

Jacob's bedroom is silent and dark. Again, the only light in the room is the monitor of his computer. The monitor shines upon a tired young man, struggling to concentrate, playing a spirited game of chess versus the machine. The light from the monitor dissipates, as it seems to be nearly completely absorbed by Jacob's face. Jacob's deep level of concentration is broken. He senses a presence, something inviting him to remove himself from the late night computer game. His once sagging eyes are bulging open with excitement and intrigue. Jacob rises, drawn to his closet for no apparent reason. He walks, with each step anticipating something great, something he has been waiting for. Jacob whips open his closet, his eyes are drawn to the carpet below. Clothes and toys line the floor of the closet posing nothing out of the ordinary.

Then, a breakthrough. Jacob's eyes are caught by a dark long leathery figure. He reaches down and clutches in his hands a black leather scabbard. A gold handle, dulled by the darkness, decorated by a cross of red jewels, stands tall out of the black casing. Jacob removes the scabbard, displaying the glory he had hoped for. A long finely sharpened sword blade awe's Jacob's entire world. He closes his eyes, thanking God for his good fortune. Upon opening his eyes, Jacob is no longer in his bedroom, or Starktown, Illinois for that matter.

Twelve

The streets are dark, oil soaked rags encased in glass are burning on poles and provide the only illumination in an otherwise sinister atmosphere. A few horses are tied to a rail in front of an old wooden tavern. The small town is reminiscent of an old spaghetti western flick: flimsy wooden structures, horses tied up on wood posts and a lone tumbleweed blowing across the street. Guilds, taverns, steel works, and a blacksmith seem to dominate the town's numerous shop fronts. The streets are mainly silent—the only folks foolish enough to wander around this late at night are stray drunkards, thieves, or extremely experienced and skilled swordsmen.

Jacob emerges from the shadows of an alley, like a hero entering a scene from a movie for the very first time.

Although he's draped in torn, ragged clothing, that of a peasant or serf, Jacob displays the confidence of Robin Hood himself. With his sword at his side, Jacob steps forward into the moonlight, a stern but earnest expression concealing any confusion he might have experienced over his new surroundings. He relishes the moment, feeling the exhilaration of becoming the hero.

"Ah! Help me!" The distant, muffled sounds of a damsel in distress grab Jacob's attention. He harnesses his fears and challenges his courage, dashing off in the direction of the echoed screams.

It's a dark alley, but Jacob feels compelled to step into the situation even though it may be an elaborate trap. With his sword drawn, Jacob edges into the darkness, prepared for all, ready for anything.

"You're not so perdy now, aren't ya?" Drake, a local thug and thief, mocks the woman. He takes a swig of his liquor, impairing his wits even further, his laughter and speech slurred to the point of becoming nearly unrecognizable.

Drake looks just like an older rugged version of Vinni, Jacob's arch enemy.

"Yeah!" Ray Hassel agrees, as usual, with his partner. Ray is taller and looks just like Casey, Jacob's other nemesis.

The woman they mock is concealed in the darkness, her legs and dress dirtied by the ground below.

The toothless, senseless, smelly criminals are thoroughly amused by their own disgusting habits. Their thick beards and smudged faces only add drama to their most evil of intentions.

"All right!" Drake shouts, halting the bout of laughter. "Now, if ya don't mind none perdy miss, we'll be takin' them jewels ya got."

Drake and Ray reach and grab at the damsel, who struggles to secure the wealth she's displaying around her neck.

"Unhand me I say!" orders the struggling woman, putting up quite a fight.

"You heard the lady!" yells Jacob, heroically stepping forward into plain sight of the two thieves.

The two men jump to attention, snapping their heads around.

Jacob, the young swordsmen in a serf's clothing, stares confidently down his sword at the two street rats.

"Well, lookie here, Ray," slurs an aggravated Drake obnoxiously. He tosses his bottle of poison away, the glass shattering on the ground. Drake reveals a villainous smile, enjoying the challenge of the young peasant. His few teeth are rotting, nearing black in color.

"Why don't you run off and play, boy. This doesn't concern you." Ray steps forward, cracking his knuckles, attempting to intimidate the smaller, younger man.

"I'm making it my concern," asserts Jacob.

"All right then, boy. Let's dance," Drake demands, looking for a fight. Drake turns to his partner in crime and the two pull out their own swords.

"About time!" The women erupts, stepping up out of the shadows. Claire, her face dirtied, her fine, hand-sewn, aristocratic dress smudged and ripped, steps nearly into the skirmish, pronouncing her presence with authority. Upon seeing Jacob, Claire looks surprised, as if expecting someone else.

Drake firmly shoves Claire back down to the ground and onto her bottom.

"Hey!" Claire shouts, again angered at the scavenger.

The two thugs circle around Jacob, grinning confidently, ready and willing to put the young boy down.

"I wish not to fight you, gentlemen," Jacob says. His confidence has not wavered in this offer, wearing a cocky grin as he attempts to keep one eye on Drake and the other on Ray.

"You hear that?" Drake scoffs. "He wishes not to fight us!" Drake and his partner laugh in tandem, staring down at the teen before them.

"I think it's most funny that he called you gentlemen," jokes Claire, staring directly at an angered Drake.

Jacob sends a smile Claire's way, amused by her wit, while continuing to keep his eyes on the two circling thieves. The two thieves ponder the insult and have trouble recognizing it.

"Hey!" Drake finally realizes he has been insulted by the fine maiden.

"You actually didn't let me finish," states Jacob to the two angry men. "As I was saying. I wish not to fight you, for I do not believe in the art of war, but if you insist, I will kill you both."

"It's two against one, boy!" Drake points out the obvious with the utmost confidence. Ray chuckles too, siding with his good buddy, but the laughter is nervous. The two men try to remain as cocky and confident as their street mentality has taught them, but, inside, they are no sword fighters. And if there's one thing they know about this young man, it's that he means business.

"No," proclaims Jacob. "It is two against an army, for I fight with the heart of a hundred men. I am Jacob of the West and I have fought for those of lesser fortunes all my life. I have slain the mightiest of dragons and outlasted the best of swordsmen. And I say to you gentlemen here tonight, if you wish to fight me, you will die at the very places you stand right at this moment. Prepare to die!" Jacob hurls the torch down as if it were a gauntlet and raises his sword in dramatic fashion, ready to battle and defeat the two men.

Drake and Ray, both intimidated, showing much hesitation, race to find a rational thought in their heads. Scared and knowing they are outmatched, the two men dash off down the alley into darkness.

Jacob turns his attentions to Claire, the fair maiden. Her face is lit up by the heroic actions of her savior.

"Thank you, kind sir," states Claire with an interested and intrigued glow about her expression. Her eyes gaze at the young hero, asking a thousand and one questions about his existence in her life. "You're quite a man," she compliments with an abundance of sincerity.

"Just a man. But they, they were thieving cowards. It was my pleasure miss," Jacob, ever the cool collected hero, responds.

Claire paces around Jacob with a playful smile on her face. "I've heard of you," she declares. "They call you 'Jacob the Great,' do they not?" Jacob nods in agreement.

"You help the poor and accept nothing for yourself. You are a humble great man and you do exist in more than just dreams." Claire speaks of the young man as if he were a mystical fable, a figment of some child's hopeful imagination.

"That I am, miss," Jacob bows gracefully before Claire. "What might your name be?" "Claire." The word rolls off her lips like melted chocolate, so warm, sweet, and pure.

"No last name?" asks Jacob, his eyes filled with intrigue.

"Just Claire," she responds, again with that same playful grin.

"All right then…Just Claire. It is an honor to meet such a beautiful soul out here amongst the dirt and filth. You are an angel amid demons."

"My goodness," responds a breathless and overtaken Claire. "You've made me blush!"

Claire backs away toward the street entrance, gazing back at her knight in shining armor. Jacob remains in his alley, watching as the mysterious Claire exits his life as abruptly as she entered.

"Is this to be it?" Jacob dramatically asks himself, his mind infatuated with Claire. "My heart is touched for the first time, and now the most beautiful creature I've ever laid my eyes upon is fleeing away from me. Is this a quandary or a blessing?"

Claire suddenly stops at the mouth of the alley and slowly turns back to Jacob. "Fear not mighty warrior, for we will meet again. I swear it."

And like that, Claire is gone, wishing kind words upon Jacob as if reading his thoughts.

"I have found my true love," Jacob states to himself with a subtle tone and a heavy heart.

Thirteen

The sun is breaking free of the horizon's grip. Clouds left over from the cold night are streaking across the broad sky, leaving blotches of blue. The light peeks through Jacob's blinds, providing ample illumination in the room. The young boy lies fast asleep on the floor, still dressed in the clothing he wore the night before. His hands are clutching something beneath his body, sheltered from the light of day.

"Wake up, Jake!" Ryan's stern voice sounds from high above Jacob's unconscious body.

Ryan shakes his head at his passed out brother and reaches down to shake him out of his deep slumber. Upon the touch of just one of his fingers, Jacob springs to his feet, wielding the aluminum bat that was hidden underneath his body. He flashes the bat around like a sword in his hands. Jacob's angry and concentrated expression forces Ryan backward, ill prepared for the sudden outburst.

"Are you challenging me, scoundrel?" shouts Jacob, continuing to swing the bat around, narrowly missing Ryan's face.

"Snap out of it, Jacob!" a retreating Ryan orders, his eyes fixed on the threatening bat.

Jacob steps forward, his eyes concentrated on the blade of his sword as it shines in the morning sun's rays. The glowing sword reassures him of the intensity of the moment.

"Unhand the fair maiden!" Jacob shouts back, all the while cutting through the air with his sword, forcing Ryan into a corner.

Ryan runs out of room and trips over a pile of Jacob's toys and clothes, falling back into the closet.

Jacob rushes over to Ryan, holding the edge of his shiny blade up against his neck, preparing for a fatal blow if his demands are not met.

Ryan knocks the bat away from his neck, not amused by his brother's shenanigans.

"Jesus, Jacob!" Ryan barks at his little brother.

Jacob stares down at his hands, realizing he's holding an aluminum bat. His eyes had played tricks on him, but how? He thought it was truly a sword. He slowly backs away, confused over his whereabouts. He sees his computer, his clock, bed, dirty clothes on the ground. Yes, this is his bedroom, but it does not seem like home.

Embarrassed, Jacob blushes, looking down to the ground, embarrassed by his perplexing display.

"Sorry," a sincerely apologetic Jacob mumbles, not quite sure what came over him.

Ryan rises to his feet, recognizing his brother's remorse.

"Billy's downstairs, Zorro," Ryan mumbles.

Jacob's head hangs low, a sight not often seen. The boy is outspoken, outlandish, and an introvert fighting to be an extrovert, but this level of confusion never overtakes him. His life has been free-willed, but calculated within the deepest depths of his mind. This incident was not.

Ryan senses the turmoil brewing inside his younger brother.

"Hey, Jake, you okay?" Ryan shows a touch of concern.

"Yeah, I'm…I'm all right," Jacob mumbles, still a bit hazy inside.

"Okay," nods a satisfied Ryan, the answer good enough for him.

Jacob slowly sets the bat down against a wall and drags himself past Ryan, exiting the bedroom.

Ryan stares at Jacob, worrisome over his mental state. "He's getting worse," the words echo inside Ryan's head like a bad song. Ryan takes a deep breath and follows his little sib out of the bedroom.

Ring...ring...

"Hello?" A tired and groggy Claire answers her phone. She brushes her hair out of her eyes, as if that will help her speak to whomever has awaken her in the early morning hours.

"Sweetheart? How are you, dear?" Claire's mother, nearly a thousand miles away in distance, but never far enough, asks.

"Mom? What time is it?" Claire rolls over, searching for the time.

"It's early dear. How are you feeling? How was the move?" The questions fly out like bullets.

Claire's face drops. The last thing she wants to deal with this morning is her mother.

"Everything's fine, Mom. I left all the information on your machine. It's…it's all good, okay."

"I know dear. You're my Claire, baby."

"Oh, Mom, don't call me that." Claire groans, setting her hand on her forehead, attempting to head off any ensuing migraine.

"How is Starksville? Everything you hoped for, dear?"

"Starktown, Mom," corrects Claire, becoming annoyed with her intrusive mother.

"Sorry, dear, it's just so hard to keep up with your moves."

"I've only moved twice, mom. Once from the house to Chicago. And now, from Chicago to here," Claire points out, taking offense to her mother's insinuation.

"Yes, but dear, you're still a young woman. That's a lot of moving for a young woman. And have you spoken with Derek yet?"

"Derek?" Claire's ears and head perk up, her mother pinching a nerve.

"Did you tell him where you moved to?"

"Mother, I told you, it's over. It's been over. He's moved on and so have I. There is no Derek anymore."

"I just think it's a shame you moved from Chicago just because…" "Mother!" Claire interrupts, asserting her authority in the matter.

"All right, I don't know who said a mother can't be concerned."

I wish more people, at this point, Claire thinks, but the words never make it to her mouth.

"Are you all settled in there?" her mother continues.

Claire pans her eyes across her loft. Boxes are strewn across the room, making the floor boards disappear. A small bed, a coffee table with a box of tissues and a cup of water, and her phone are all this loft is prepared to offer anyone.

"Yeah. I'm all set up," Claire lies, not wanting to deal with any more of her mother's worries.

"How's the job?"

"Good." Claire's answers are short and abrupt, wanting this conversation to have ended what seems like days ago.

"Change is never good, dear. Change is so much harder than just keeping things the way they ought to be." Claire's mother offers her the wisdom of her own lifetime, for better or for worse.

"Sure, Mom, whatever you say." Claire firmly disagrees, but lacks the enthusiasm and the strength to argue with her.

"Bad weather's gonna be comin' your way next week, dear. Be ready for it. Get back out that winter coat. You're gonna need it."

"Okay, Mom. Okay."

Fourteen

Martin, Stan, Carlos, and Ryan are carrying boards of wood into the house which is looking more and more like a place of residence than a skeletal exterior of what might be. Their foreheads are glistening from hours of work in the mid-morning sun. They are lucky though—the clouds, the giant pillows which are sporadically floating throughout the sky, have been pretty good about limiting the heat and sunlight available to the earth on this crisp late spring day.

They carry the boards over to the would-be staircase, resting them down atop an already flourishing pile of wood.

"So what happened with you and the mamacita last night, amigo?" Carlos questions, the first of the men to break on the subject.

All four men smile, knowing full well this brand of locker room chatter was inevitable. Ryan even adds a chuckle as he turns and leaves the other three men waiting for his highly anticipated response. The boys hurry after him, following Ryan back outside for answers.

"Yeah, come on, Ryno. You gotta tell us," Stan says, relying on the rules of friendship.

All four men stop in their tracks upon seeing Claire's BMW parked in front of the house. The beautiful young woman herself steps out of the car, but she isn't alone this morning. Mrs. Flowers, a respected and feared woman in town, exits the passenger's seat. Mrs. Flowers has managed to beat cancer and survived the death of three husbands. She shot a man once—an ex-husband who had a few bad habits. Turns out, drinking and physical abuse do not go together in Mrs. Flowers's world. But that's an old story from ancient history. Now, Mrs. Flowers has found her true love and they're building a home together from scratch.

"This ain't no locker room boys. Stand to attention, Flowers has arrived." Ryan commands of his troops.

"Gentlemen." Not a ferocious greeting from one of Starktown's oldest treasures, but one that sends chills down the men's backs.

"Ma'am," they respectively return to Mrs. Flowers, as she and Claire move down the walkway towards the house.

Ryan and Claire's eyes meet, sharing a short but sweet smile.

The two women enter the developing home, one which is starting to take on great shape and hope.

"You are well worth your reputation Mr. Crestwood." These are Mrs. Flowers's only words, and a rare compliment to the workmen. She and Claire continue on by themselves for a tour of the house.

"Gentlemen, please!" Martin clears the other men away from Ryan, demanding his best friend's privacy be respected. Martin leads Ryan over to the flatbed of his truck. As Ryan reaches inside for a red toolbox, Martin attacks.

"All right, man, tell me what happened," urges Martin.

"What?" Ryan laughs at his friend over his own personal agenda to gain an unfair informational advantage over everyone else. "What happened to the privacy of a friend and all that other crap?"

"Come on, man! I need to hear about this bachelor stuff," begs Martin, appearing desperate for any kind of news on the subject. "You know I'm trapped forever in the chains of matrimonial hell. You and 'Los are my only way of tasting the good life."

"What about Stan?" Ryan sarcastically asks.

"Come on, Ryan, I'm not joking with you right now!"

"The good life? What else is there if I'm living 'the good life'?" Ryan asks with a slant of sarcasm.

"Marriage…the dark side," whispers Martin ominously, spoken like a man who has seen the devil.

"Get out of here! You and Joanne are great together! Don't give me that!" Ryan heaves back at the exaggerating Martin.

"Yeah, but you haven't seen her in the morning. She gets all this phlegm stuck in her throat durin' the night and when she wakes up and talks…holy Jesus! She sounds just like Darth Vader." Martin continues his parade of embellishment. "Martin, get me water…now!" Martin deepening his voice like some kind of chaotically evil warlord. "And her hair, her hair looks all nappy like James Brown! I wake up to a Vader soundin' James Brown every mornin' man! Now please! Please give me what I *need!*" Martin dramatically finishes off his rant.

"Okay-okay! Keep for voice down for Christ's sake." Ryan prepares himself, leaning in close to Martin, as if he were about to tell him who shot JFK. "It went…well," Ryan looks Martin seriously in the eye and nods.

Martin holds still, waiting for something more.

Ryan, satisfied and amused, leaves his friend standing empty handed and laughs all the while, heading back into the construction site carrying his red tool box.

"Oh, damn, Ryan! Come on, man!" Martin, his face wrinkled up in disappointment. He's a child that got absolutely nothing but an empty box on Christmas and wants to pout about it. "Why ya gonna play me like that?" Martin shouts at deaf ears, marching back over to presumably get some work done.

Ryan enters the kitchen, where Claire is in the midst of giving Mrs. Flowers a tour of the place.

"Hello, Mr. Crestwood. Things are coming together," Mrs. Flowers comments.

"Yes, ma'am. We're gonna have you living here in no time."

Mrs. Flowers looks over the kitchen in-process, and winces. "I hope not too soon," she comments sarcastically.

"We're getting there," adds Claire, tossing Ryan a flotation device.

"Yes…well, I'm going to head upstairs and review the progress there," Mrs. Flowers states, on her way to the freshly built wood stairs.

"I'll be up in a minute," Claire alerts Mrs. Flowers.

Ryan takes a step closer to Claire, seizing the moment.

"I had a great time last night," he comments, tilting his head down to the ground like a nervous school boy. The sight is precious, and Claire smiles, amused by the genuine innocence.

"Me too," Claire agrees. "You know what I feel like doing?" Claire's eyes shimmer with excitement.

"What?" Ryan asks hanging on Claire's every word.

"I feel like taking a walk through the oak forest just as the sun is setting behind the trees. That's when you can actually smell the spring in the air. The cool crisp air sweeps in from the east, shoving the warm sunshine back to the west. We have to take advantage before it gets hot. The cool weather is going to be gone soon. Then, as the night grows colder, curling up on a soft comfy couch underneath a warm blanket, and sipping hot coca, with a friendly fire burning in the fire place. And we can rent a nice movie to watch."

"Wow, that was a big what," Ryan jokes with a quirky smile. "I like that a lot." He grows serious in the moment.

"You think I could join you?"

"Maybe." Claire smiles sprightly, now acting the school girl playing hard to get.

"Your place?" Ryan offers, wanting to stay as far away from his own house as possible.

"Actually, my apartment's still not quite settled in yet. Let's do it at your house. It's nice and homey there," Claire compliments.

"Sure, that sounds great," the hesitance is obvious in Ryan's voice, his nerves over another late night battle with Jacob already haunting him.

Claire smiles and happily heads off, leaving a now concerned Ryan behind.

———◆———

Doctor Wells spends what little free time he has in his office. The room is dark, very comfortable, with his desk hand fashioned in solid oak with a dark liquor finish. The finely glossed desk is accompanied by a matched set of solid oak chairs, each facing the broad oak fixture. The walls are lined with various medical degrees and eclectic ink paintings, many of which look like strange blobs of black pen, resembling nothing and everything at the same time. Doctor Wells is seated in a dark red recliner, it too bordered with a fine oak finish. Lying on the maroon colored couch is Jacob. His feet are propped up on one of the arms while his head is resting comfortably on a white cotton pillow.

"Jacob, I don't want you to be nervous. Feel free to say whatever's on your mind." Doctor Wells' voice is relaxed and comforting, wanting Jacob to reach out, extend away from his inner shell.

Jacob's eyes are wandering about the office, his mind only partially paying attention to the good doctor.

"I like this couch. We need a new couch at home. I don't really like ours…it's old. This one—this one seems new," Jacob comments with an apparent couch fetish.

"You and Ryan doing okay?" Doctor Wells feels the need to jump-start the question and answer session.

"Sure." Jacob again retreats to a typical one-word answer.

"What do you guys talk about on an average day? Ya know, you're both lounging around on a Saturday, maybe watching the Bears game, what do you guys talk about?" Doctor Wells asks, more specifically.

"Can I sit up on the couch? I mean, am I allowed to, or would it be against the rules? Because I see in movies all the nutso people have to stay subdued on their backs in the stereotypical patient-on-psychiatrist's-couch scene. They never seem to sit up. I always wonder if that's their decision or if the doctor doesn't let them." Jacob rambles on and on, avoiding any real emotional or personal subject matter.

"Of course. If you'd like to sit up, go ahead and do it. Be comfortable, Jacob," Doctor Wells plays along, curious where Jacob will take the conversation next.

"Cool." Jacob sits up and remains quiet, shifting his body around, quite uncomfortable with the spotlight shining directly upon him.

"Jacob, do you think you're nutso?" Doctor Wells uses one of Jacob's own words.

"I don't know. I think I'm different in my own way. It's better to be original than ordinary, right?"

"That's a good question, Jake. I believe that you are a very original soul and that is a very good thing. But ordinary and originality, that's all subjective to people. Those questions aren't so black and white. But I wanna get back to discussing you and Ryan. What do you boys talk about at home?"

"I don't know. We just talk about stuff. He tells me when Billy comes over or he tries to make sure I have stuff to do. He takes care of me, I guess." Jacob's melancholy tone strikes Doctor Wells as interesting.

"You guys do a lot of stuff together? Go camping, toss the ball around—ya know, guys stuff?"

"Sometimes…not usually though. I do stuff with Billy. He and I fish and hang out together most of the time.

He also has a crush on Cara—but don't tell him I told you. I think I'm gonna help him out with that."

"Yes. You and Billy are best friends," Doctor Wells says, smiling, like a warm uncle. "How about your mom? You told me you thought she was nutso." Doctor Wells continues to hammer away at Jacob, slowly but surely trying to break down his mile high walls.

"You know she is, Doc Wells. You take care of her," Jacob says.

"Yes, I do," Doctor Wells smiles, amused by Jacob pointing out the obvious. "Do you think you're more like her or somebody else in your family?"

"I'd say…I'm probably more like her than my dad or Ryan."

"How so?" Doctor Wells is legitimately curious how Jacob may answer this vital question, leaning in to hear his response.

"My mom does things because they feel right. She used to act the way she did because inside, something told her that life was fun. She loved being spontaneous. That's what I loved most about her. She's always told me that happiness above all else was most important. And Dad and Ryan are strict and responsible. They live their life by rules. I don't think they like life much—at least Ryan doesn't seem to. That's why my dad died. I don't think he cared enough about living." The sincerity in Jacob's thoughts is striking to Doctor Wells.

"You think your father passed away because he didn't want to live anymore."

"That's what he told me."

"That's what who told you?" Doctor Wells' brow furrows.

"My dad," Jacob states.

"Before he died?"

"No, in my dreams," Jacob says, so frank and forthright, as if this kind of behavior is normal.

Doctor Wells sits back, realizing he's stumbled upon a whole other session of material. The good doctor knows how special this boy truly is, but how destructive might he actually become?

Jacob exits Doctor Wells' office. Patiently waiting on the floor of the hallway is Billy. Billy hops up to his feet, excited to see his best friend finished with his Q and A session.

"Come on Jake, can we finally go play now?" Billy begs, wanting so badly to release the mounds of energy he has built up inside him.

"All right." Jacob's focus remains on the questions Doctor Wells posed to him. He is surrounded by his thoughts, but shows little signs that the session actually had an effect on him. Everything is kept inside. Everything is always kept inside. Although Jacob carries the outward appearance of an extrovert, inside he is a web of complicated emotions and thoughts. Jacob is a loner in the truest sense of the word.

Jacob and Billy exit Starktown's skyscraper to see Cara pulling up on her dirty bike. It is forest green and beat up, showing the signs of years of rough riding. She takes her skull and cross boned helmet and holds it by her side, equally surprised to see Billy and Jacob.

Billy and Cara's eyes have trouble staying off the ground.

Despite being in his own personal emotional haze, Jacob recognizes Cara and Billy's levels of discomfort and he snaps out of his own clouded mind. He rises above his shackled mind and emerges to help his best friend. "What was that, Billy?" Jacob says.

"Huh?" Billy is caught off guard.

"Good idea," Jacob responds, carrying on a conversation for the two of them.

"What?" Cara asks.

"Billy asked if you could come hang out today." Jacob tosses out there.

Cara looks up and smiles at Billy, a smile that Billy catches with his own eyes. An eruption of heat and excitement tingle from Billy's belly all the way through the tips of his toes and fingers.

"Yeah," Billy musters up the courage to confirm the invitation to Cara.

"I would like to…,"Cara begins, with hope emerging.

Billy's eyes widen with excitement. Jacob, for a moment, feels as though he successfully confirmed the love connection.

"But I have to stay here for a while, and then my mom is taking me to see my aunt and uncle near Chicago. We'll be gone the night," Cara, as deflated as the boys, completes the bad news.

"Next time," Billy offers.

Those two words, *next time*, bring about a proud smile from Jacob. Jacob is staring over at Billy in utter shock. It's as if his best friend just conquered the world with those two little words. Billy's confident rise to speak to a girl, a girl he *likes*, is nothing less than extraordinary to Jacob.

"Thanks," Cara says.

And with that, their two sets of eyes once again find the ground.

Jacob's mood has rebounded with a thunderous smile, he watches as Cara and Billy's connection is unarguably cemented.

"Bye," Cara smirks and moves past the boys.

"Bye," Jacob and Billy say in unison as the girl enters the building.

Jacob turns to Billy with his big smile still plastered across his face.

"What?" Billy responds to Jacob's undeniable change in mood.

"You know what," Jacob continues to smile at Billy.

"Come on," Billy moves the conversation along, not wanting to dwell further in his new budding relationship.

The two friends grab their bikes and start to ride off, the smell of victory following their every pedal down the road.

Fifteen

The world is darker than it should be at this time in the late afternoon. The sun is temporarily shielded by a few of those puffy cumuli drifting slowly high up in the sky. There is a hint of anger amongst the clouds, a sign of harsher weather to come.

Ryan enters through the front door of his house like any other day, unsure of what he'll find. Upon opening the door after his long day of hammering, lifting boards of wood, and sweating up a smelly storm, he is met by a plastic hockey ball flying at the tip of his nose. He flinches back, the ball not quite as close to his face as he first thought, but close enough. The ball deflects off the wall, and like two hungry hockey thugs, Jacob and Billy, dressed in full pads, netted hockey jerseys, and football helmets, fly by on roller blades, grabbing at one another as they chase after the loose ball. Ryan watches in amazement, unsure of what he should say.

Billy reaches the ball first, trying to shield Jacob away with his body. Jacob lightly checks Billy into the wall, letting him know that he shouldn't expect to get out of this corner clean. One check, then another, and finally, on the third, Billy loses his balance and eats it, falling down to the ground.

Jacob's electrified, pouncing on the loose ball and skating back by Ryan into the living room. Billy chases after him, a dopey, excited smile on his face. The two boys seem to be having the time of their lives.

Ryan on the other hand, is suffering from an ongoing nightmare. He closes the door behind him and follows the boys into the living room; or what once was the living room. All of the furniture and items in the living room have been packed into one stuffy corner. The room is unrecognizable, as if a tornado came through and spun everything out of control. Ryan's jaw drops. The stress of Claire coming over for the evening was enough, now he had to deal with a quick remodel of the living room before she makes her way over.

"Jacob!" Ryan shouts angrily.

Jacob and Billy, their bodies bouncing off one another, again checking for the plastic ball, stop in their places.

They look up like two children who got caught with their hands in the cookie jar.

"What do you think you're doing here?" Ryan tries his best to remain rational and calm.

Jacob stays silent for a moment, thinking long and hard about Ryan's question. Meanwhile, Billy loses his balance and tumbles down to the ground. Jacob snickers for a moment, as does Billy, a little embarrassed. Jacob helps his smaller friend back on top of his blades, aiding his balance.

Ryan shakes his head, growing more and more impatient by the second. Inside he's fuming. What should he do? What should he say? His brother doesn't know any better. How can he punish his younger brother when he doesn't know any better?

"I'm sorry, what did you ask?" Jacob tentatively asks.

Ryan has every reason to become infuriated, but maintains his sanity. He takes a deep breath and again tries.

"What are you two doing?" Gritting his teeth, he resists the temptation to explode.

"It's not what it looks like," Jacob comes to his and Billy's defense.

"So you're not playing roller hockey in the house?" Ryan asks his younger brother frustrated.

"Oh. I guess it is what it looks like then. But to our defense, you are kinda home early," Jacob politicizes, citing a reason for why the house is a mess.

Ryan, hoping for a better answer than that, runs his hands through his hair, using all internal meanings of restraint to hold himself back from letting out a barrage of angry four letter words.

"Move everything back," he says—a simple yet direct order given by the master of the house. Ryan turns to head upstairs and take a warm, much needed shower.

"Can we finish the period?" Jacob asks, now trying to finagle as much time as possible out of his frustrated brother. Any other person would probably lay back and abide by the laws of the land. Not Jacob. He knows how far he can push his brother.

Ryan stops in his tracks and rolls his neck, not wanting to deal with the situation any more. "How much time's left in the period?" Ryan humors the boys.

"Billy?" Jacob turns to his trusty friend.

Billy looks down at his watch and almost loses his balance again, scissoring his feet back and forth. After a moment or two, he's able to keep his balance.

"About one-hundred and thirty five minutes…give or take a minute," Billy precisely states.

"You got ten minutes," Ryan lays down the law. He straggles up the stairs, not wanting to deal with all this extra stress.

"How about fifteen?" Jacob again tries to pull on the puppet strings, every minute counting to him.

"Ten!" Ryan grumbles angrily, not even turning back to acknowledge Jake's counter offer.

"Damn," Jacob mutters to himself, knowing he and Billy only have a short time to play.

"Boy, he's pissy today," Billy points out to Jacob, the two sharing in their game-time frustrations.

Jacob and Billy look at one another, thinking about what to do next. With little hesitation, Jacob lightly cross checks Billy, knocking him on his back, and takes the puck, skating off around the house. Billy struggles to his feet with a big smile on his face and chases after his best friend. The two boys disappear into the kitchen, skating and spreading their fun all around the house. They giggle and laugh, the best friends having the time of their lives.

The oak forest at sunset is one of the most romantic natural features around Starktown. The surrounding forest contains many cardinals, all of whom are racing about the tree-tops attempting to find their perfect mates.

Hand in hand, Ryan and Claire, each dressed comfortably casual for the night, stroll through the dusk of the day amongst the prehistoric giants.

"So, tell me your life story," Claire demands with a smirk on her face, knowing full well the question could never be answered with a mere sentence.

"My life story?" Ryan gasps, nearly choking on the question.

"Yeah, why not?" Claire playfully smiles.

"You first. What's your life story?" Ryan sends the question back into Claire's court, needing a bar set for his own answer.

"Okay, I'll go first," Claire agrees. "My father died when I was thirteen. I had to help my mom raise my two younger sisters, taking away from my teenage years. I didn't get to screw around as a kid, but what can you do when your family needs you? I grew up quickly—I had to. I became chained to the house, and subsequently, I have had problems sustaining what some might call a *successful* relationship," Claire jests with the full weight of sincerity behind her joking.

Ryan stares at Claire as if he's looking into a mirror. The path her life has taken her is oddly familiar to the role he himself was forced to take with Jacob.

"What's that look for?" Claire's a little weirded out by Ryan's penetrating stare.

"It's like looking into a mirror from the past. I'm not only Jake's brother, but I've had to play father too, since I was sixteen."

"Really? What happened?" Claire becomes increasingly interested.

Ryan calms himself, his excitement level dropping upon Claire's request. He's not sure what to say, or how to derail this conversation.

"It's just that…" Ryan struggles to find an answer he can live with and one that Claire won't think is too strange.

"Did I strike a nerve?" Claire recognizes Ryan's hesitancy.

"It's just the past. I was real close with my father when he passed away. Jacob was real young and I wasn't old enough—at least I didn't think so. I was around the same age you were when your dad died. I had to pick up the slack around the house." Ryan is glum in his description of the past. A sadness prevails in his voice, leaving Claire empathetic.

"You gave up a lot to help your mother."

"To say the least," Ryan says, with a touch of sarcasm and laced with bitterness.

The two walk silently, both pondering their rough childhood.

"So tell me," Ryan begins, changing the subject. "How'd you end up in Starktown?" Ryan starts in on his own quest of curiosity.

"A nice job," Claire dances, like a fighter avoiding a right hook.

"Did I strike a nerve?" Ryan parrots Claire, grinning.

"Let's just say you're not the only one with some skeletons in their closet," Claire returns Ryan's grin with one of her own.

Ryan stops walking and Claire follows his lead, the two looking off into the remaining half of the sun slowly being dragged down below the horizon. Claire runs her hand along the side of Ryan's face, touching more than just his clean-shaven face. Ryan lights up inside, an eruption of warmth running through his body. Ryan smiles and places his arm around the angelic creature's waist. The two stand together, a beautiful postcard of romance. They stare at the sunset, their bodies' side-by-side.

The late night plans have led the budding couple back to the Crestwood couch for an evening by the fire. A nice hand-knitted wool blanket is draped over their legs and bodies, Claire cozying up close to Ryan for some extra warmth. The fire is warming up the room further, setting the romantic mood to a tee. The lights are off and "Titanic", obviously Claire's choice of movie, is sinking on the television screen.

Hiding on the dark stairway are Jacob and Billy, lying on their bellies as if they were in the jungles of Vietnam.

Jacob is looking through a pair of binoculars and sees Claire snuggling up to the evil Ryan, a scowl producing deep resentment inside the young man's belly. Billy on the other hand is looking through a telescope, unable to recognize anything except for a couple of blurred dark figures.

"I can't see anything," Billy complains, frustrated by his lackluster view.

Jacob glances over and pulls the telescope out of Billy's hands.

"Here, look through this," Jacob whispers, handing Billy the binoculars.

"Wow, she's pretty hot," Billy witnesses Claire pulling even closer to Ryan.

"Hey, watch it!" Jacob sternly whispers, smacking Billy in the shoulder. Jacob grabs the binoculars away from Billy, not liking his point of view on the matter.

"Geez, sorry," Billy apologizes, never seeing this side of Jacob.

"We goin' fishing on Saturday?" Billy asks.

"Sure," Jacob pays little attention to his friend, fixing the binoculars back over his eyes.

"Maybe Cara can come too?" Billy reaches out for additional assistance from his friend.

"Yeah, whatever. We'll make it happen," Jacob replies, still not focusing on what Billy is saying.

Jacob stares through the looking glass, a nightmare becoming reality. Claire slowly leans in towards Ryan's lips, their eyes entangled within one another. Ryan slowly leans down, their eyes closing, their lips about to touch for the very first time.

"Oh, boy!" Jacob says, nervously.

"*Achoo!*" Jacob lets out a fake sneeze, shocking the moment.

Claire and Ryan snap their heads over to the stairs, caught off guard by the random, untimely sneeze. They see nothing, and satisfied, Claire turns back to watching the movie. Ryan on the other hand glares at the staircase suspiciously, knowing full well that was no accidental, random sneeze. After a few more moments, Ryan gives up his concentrated optical scan and turns his attention back to Claire and the movie.

An hour later, Ryan and Claire remain in the same positions on the couch. Their cuddling is reminiscent of a long time couple share one of many moments of love with one another.

And then two pairs of legs come charging down the stairs.

Ryan and Claire once again are distracted from the evening, spinning their heads around to see what's going on.

"I'm going to ride with Billy back to his house!" Jacob blurts out, again trying to play spoiler against the romantic moment.

"Okay." Ryan is happy to see Jacob and Billy finally go.

"Hi, Billy. I'm Claire." Her subtle, soft words embarrass the shyest of the shy.

Billy looks down to the ground, rolling his right foot around on the ground, becoming increasingly fidgety. "Billy doesn't talk much." Jacob speaks up for his shy friend, always coming to his protection.

"Okay, well…it was nice meeting you, Billy."

Billy smiles and nods to Claire, glancing up for just a moment. The second his eyes make contact with Claire's he shoots them back down at the ground.

Jacob opens up the door, allowing Billy to slide out first.

"Ride safely," Claire offers a kind sentiment to the boys.

A shot of adrenaline races through Jacob's loins. Claire had kind words for him. The two compassionate words play over and over again, injecting Jacob with a glimpse of hope. He closes the door behind him, feeling oddly excited.

Ryan and Claire rise from the couch, both stretching their arms and backs, while the credits role on the television.

"Where's the rest room?"

"You have to use the one upstairs. It's just to the left," Ryan directs.

"Thanks." Claire dashes up the stairs, heading up toward the Crestwood lair. Claire hops up off the top step and freezes in the place she stands, a sight of extreme intrigue overwhelming her. She's staring at the gateway to Jacob's bedroom. The door is covered in those numerous news articles dealing with Los Angeles. Claire stares at the door, wondering, why and what does this mean? Who would do such a thing to the outside of their bedroom door? Claire reaches out, frightened of what might happen if she actually touches this strange door.

The door is ever so gently nudged forward with thoughts of a possible booby-trap awaiting any unwanted visitors. Claire slides her body into the unknown world of this fascinating young boy. She searches the wall near the entrance and finds a light switch. She flips the lights on, expecting nothing and everything all at once. Her eyes and thoughts do not deceive her. She gets everything. The room has so many things to look at for a stranger. It all comes together now. The room and even the outside of the door are all representations of the city of Los Angeles. Not just an item or two, but a room filled with trinkets, paraphernalia, an entire surreal world. Posters, banners, everything down to the tiniest of details. The room looks more envious of a dwelling for a cartoon character rather than a human being.

Claire jumps as Ryan knocks on the door behind her, the knocking reaching down into the world she had fallen into and pulling her back into reality.

"Oh, I'm sorry," Claire apologizes, a little embarrassed to be caught snooping around.

"Don't be," Ryan, standing at the door, panning his eyes around the room at all of Jacob's oddities. "If I walked by this room, I'd be looking in it myself," Ryan agrees with Claire, but for far different reasons.

"He seems to be quite fond of Los Angeles," Claire points out the obvious.

"It's LA month," Ryan sarcastically states, with a wealth of seriousness behind his jesting.

"Yeah?" Claire lets out a short gasp, oddly fascinated by Ryan's assessment.

"I think next month's New York, but I never know exactly what Jacob's going to do," Ryan displays his frustrations and confusions in dealing with his strange younger brother. As the phone rings downstairs, Ryan lets out an annoyed breath of air, turning about.

"Excuse me," Ryan says politely, asking Claire to excuse the intrusive ambiguous soul on the other line of the telephone. Ryan exits Jacob's bedroom, heading down the hall to his own bedroom.

Claire goes back to touring around the extraordinary domicile.

"Hello?" Ryan quickly asks of the caller, wanting to return to the most attractive woman he has ever watched a late night movie with.

"What's up, brother?!" An excited Martin calls, wanting nothing more than dirt on the tone of the evening.

Ryan drags the phone line away from the wall searching the hall for Claire. He sees only the light from Jacob's bedroom leaking into the hallway.

"Can I call you back, dog? I'm kinda busy right now." Ryan is distracted and obsessed with the whereabouts of his date.

"She's still there, isn't she?" Martin devilishly chuckles, hoping for some sexual information.

Claire strolls over to Jacob's desk, a single piece of paper filled with recently inked words resting all by itself. Claire glances over her shoulder, making sure she's alone. Satisfied she has her privacy, Claire turns back to the single sheet of paper. Claire takes a seat and begins to read:

THE INVISIBLE MAN
Oh, what it would be like to be invisible.
To be able to sneak in and out whenever you wanted; never to be spotted.
To go places where once you were forbidden to enter.
To be whoever you wanted without hassle.
It would be so great to be invisible.
Just think of it. The freedom,

The solitude,
The time to spend with your own thoughts without interruption.
You could take whatever you want and nobody would know.
You could get everything; you could be anything.
It would be absolutely blissful.
And then one day it happened.
I became invisible.
I walked everywhere I had ever wanted to walk.
I traveled everywhere I had ever wanted to travel.
I did it all.
I did it all without anyone knowing.
I was invisible.
Then, things changed.
I became lonely; disgruntled and annoyed by my sea of privacy.
Being invisible was no longer a dream, but a curse.
I began to choke on my own thoughts.
My ideas consumed me and only me.
They built up inside my head and began to push on my skull.
I could feel my head expanding.
I felt as if I was about to explode.
The silence rang in my ears like a fire alarm.
I couldn't see.
Now, no longer could I go everywhere.
No longer could I see everything. Now I was blind.
I was blind and no one could find me.
I was alone in the dark with nothing.
I was invisible.
  By Jacob

"The Invisible Man," Jacob comments, breaking Claire's concentrated trance.

She spins around, abruptly standing up from the desk, again caught red-handed.

"I hope it was okay for me to…" Claire, worrisome, attempts to explain.

"I have no secrets," Jacob declares, cutting Claire off in mid explanation.

"It's quite good," Claire refers to the poem, impressed by the dramatic and gripping nature of the piece.

"Really?" Jacob is stirred by Claire's kind words. A beautiful woman has read his work, the beautiful woman he loves. This is amazing! It's the first time anyone has read one of his works, and it was Claire, his mysterious angelic beauty.

"Yeah, it's so passionate and real," Claire comments genuinely. The piece enthralled her, taking her to another place, another level of reality.

"Would you like to see some more?" Jacob steps forward, more excited than ever.

"I'd love to," Claire agrees, expecting another poem of two to be set into her hands.

Jacob shows some hop in his steps, rushing over to a corner of his room where some clothes had piled up. He tosses the clothes one by one revealing an old treasure chest. He unlocks and opens the box, staring down at his most prized possessions. Jacob signals Claire to step over to the chest.

She slowly moves over, unsure of what to expect. Upon approaching the chest, she sees with her eyes, thousands upon thousands of pieces of paper, in no set order, resting inside the old lock box. Her eyes light up in amazement, unaware of the extent of Jacob's writing.

"My goodness," the words short of breath tumble out of Claire's mouth, uncertain of what to say.

"Will you read all of them?" The bright-eyed Jacob pleads for a *yes* with his eyes. It's like a small boy asking his mother for the toy of a lifetime. Jacob's found the one person he trusts with his life, with his works.

"I don't think I'll be able to right now. This is absolutely amazing though." Claire sifts through some of the pages with her fingers, a different story or poem inked on every single one of the pages. "You love your writing, don't you?"

"I like to say what's on my mind and in my heart. Sometimes there's just no one you can tell it to, so I write." A response fired directly from Jacob's heart, revealing a piece of his soul he dared never show before.

"I will read every one of these," Claire promises to the boy. She swears to him like a mother to a son.

"Tonight?" Jacob unrealistically hopes.

Claire lets out a burst of laughter, knowing in no uncertain terms that this job could take days.

"No, but I will over time. I promise." Again Claire shows Jacob all the sincerity in the world.

"Cool! Great!" Jacob closes up his chest as Claire rises to her feet. She heads to the doorway of Jacob's bedroom.

"Oh, hey!" Jacob catches Claire before she can exit. "My brother and I would love if you came over Saturday afternoon." Jacob extends the offer as if he and Ryan had discussed it earlier.

"What's going on Saturday?" returns Claire curiously.

"Saturday's our mother's birthday. We're having a little party and we're going to bake a cake that day." Jacob tries to sway the enchanting creature and lure her back to the Crestwood estate any way he can.

"Okay. I think I can stop by about noon," Claire says, accepting the invitation.

"Awesome." Jacob smiles and nods, his night going far better than earlier planned.

"Alright, bye, Jacob." Claire exits the bedroom, shutting the door behind her.

"Sorry about the call," Ryan says, stepping up to Claire in the hallway.

"That's okay. I'm going to head home, though. I'm beat." "Sure. I'll walk you out."

Ryan follows Claire down the stairs over to the front door. He helps with her coat, making sure each arm safely slides into the thick winter sleeves.

"I had a great time tonight," Ryan shares with a soft, sensitive tone.

"So did I. Thank you, Ryan." Claire slowly leans in and the two share a soft gentle kiss. The kiss wasn't their first. A smooch or two during the movie made this kiss not nearly as nerve-racking as it could have been. Instead, it was just a brief romantic exchange.

"I'll see you tomorrow," Ryan says.

"Actually, I won't be back at the house until next Monday. I'm going over all the tapestries and furnishings with Mrs. Flowers. But I'll see you Saturday," Claire optimistically states.

"Saturday…yeah," Ryan, confused, is dumbfounded about what Claire happens to be talking about.

"I'm flattered you wanted me to come to your mother's birthday party." Claire tells Ryan, enchanted he'd be willing to let her meet his mother just two dates in.

"It's not quite a party," Ryan hedges, uncertain and distressed over escaping from what will inevitably be a bad situation.

Claire reaches up on her tiptoes and kisses Ryan on the cheek.

"See you, Saturday." Claire's grace and smile silence Ryan. No excuses for right now. He'll have to figure a way out of Saturday another time.

"Saturday it is." Ryan watches as Claire races out of the cold into her car. Claire gives one last wave goodbye as she drives off in her BMW. Ryan, steaming inside, waves goodbye, forcing himself to present a kind smile when all along, he's counting the seconds until he can take issue with

Jacob. Her car disappears down the street and Ryan rushes back into the house to wage war against his little brother.

"Jacob!" Ryan shouts, but maintains his composure, wanting a confession before he blows off steam.

Jacob innocently steps out of his bedroom to see what his elder brother might want.

"Yes, brother?" Jacob steps up to the banister at the edge of the upstairs hallway.

"What do you think you're doing?" Ryan expects Jacob to step up like a man and take responsibility for his actions.

"Right now I'm listening to you," Jacob replies plainly.

"You know exactly what I mean," Ryan says, taking an intensified stance.

"I thought that you'd want her to come. After all, this is your mother." Jacob still maintains his innocence, despite standing before the eyes of obvious guilt.

"Jake, we've gone out twice and had great times. I also have to work with her. It's enough that I've subjected her to this house, but now Mom too?" Ryan complains, his embarrassment over his family obvious to the extremely bright young man standing at the top of the stairs.

"By this house, you mean me," Jacob says, in an attempt to elicit guilt from his older brother. He could be playing on his emotional strings, but Ryan's last comment stung Jacob.

"You're just different than other people, Jake. I'm used to it, but I'm not sure if Claire is, or other folks that may come in from other places." Ryan tries to justify his earlier statement, feeling a bit regretful.

"Different…you mean strange." Jacob cuts through the fog straight to the truth and heart of the matter. The conversation has successfully turned one hundred and eighty degrees around in Jacob's favor. The young man, caught red handed for his premature invitation to the lovely

Claire, has now turned the tables on his older brother. It is Ryan who is now backtracking and on the run.

"No—different. You're not an average kid. There's nothing wrong with that. It makes you who you are and I'm not going to be embarrassed by that if you're not. And if it seems like I am sometimes, I'm sorry. I don't mean to be."

Jacob ponders his next move, realizing he's once again won a battle with his brother. Now he must turn to the problem at hand; the lovely Claire and her Saturday invitation.

"She's a really nice person." Jacob stays away from his true feelings, playing a moderate hands-off role in the conversation.

"Yeah…she is. I think she could be around for a real long time but we're just starting to learn about one another. I don't want her to be overwhelmed by our family's deepest darkest secrets." Ryan masks his embarrassment for his crazy mother. Jacob is no fool and can read right through his older brother's simple coded statement.

"You just have to be yourself, Ryan. Mom, me, we're part of you. You don't have that choice."

"That's not what I'm saying, Jake. I just wish you would have talked to me first. I have to work this Saturday. I won't even be home all afternoon," Ryan points out why the situation wouldn't work.

"So Claire and I will bake the cake in the afternoon and then we'll all go together to see Mom when you get home," Jacob offers up his spontaneous conclusions.

"That's fine, but you know that's not the point." Ryan tries to gain some kind of hand in the battle, but once again, has taken another giant leap back by giving Jake his way.

"Okay." Jacob realizes he's won and cops to whatever his brother is referring to.

"Okay, you understand the point, or okay, you don't really care?"

After a moment of pondering his brother's question, Jacob returns with, "Probably a little of both."

"I guess that will have to do," Ryan says, reluctant to accept Jacob's response, feels helpless in handling the situation any other way.

Sixteen

The streets of the town are filled with people. Nighttime belongs to the thugs and thieves, but the daytime belongs to the townspeople. They come out to buy and sell goods. They come out to hear the politics of the day. They come out to mingle and be merry. Daytime is a time for the mob to come together and the town folk, mainly serfs and lower-class businessmen, to enjoy the company of their leaders, those who have money and smarts.

Jacob is moving through town but notices something odd on this day. Many of the people are migrating toward a distant voice around the corner of the pub. The lower-class are flocking there as if they were thirsty animals in dire need of political verbiage. Jacob curiously follows his people to the *great* man they've all gone to listen to. He turns the corner and is struck by these words:

"We must move ahead! Together, we can make our village the strongest of any of our neighboring towns. We must look to the future! We must rebuild, and it starts here, now, today!" Ryan, dressed in his fancy aristocratic velvet cape with matching gold laced shoes, shouts out to the people.

"YEAH! RYAN THE GREAT! RYAN THE GREAT!" The crowd erupts with a cheer and then begins chanting "*Ryan the* Great" over and over again. The crowd hath been deceived.

Jacob skeptically looks on, shaking his head in disgust. He knows this man. The people see him as great, but Jacob is not fooled. He doesn't look to the future or to change. These words he speaks are lies and Jacob will not stand for such lies.

"He is a fraud!" Jacob's voice slices through the elation and pierces the ears of the great aristocratic man on stage.

Ryan's insulted eyes searches the crowd for the coward who would dare challenge him. The crowd quickly parts like the Red Sea, leaving Jacob standing in a virtual spotlight. All stare at him, awaiting his next words.

"That's right, my people, he's a fake," Jacob reconfirms, pouring salt into this freshly created verbal wound.

The mob turns back to Ryan, anxiously awaiting his response.

Like all good politicians, the wealthy man smiles, showcasing his pearly off-whites, more than any other man in town could show off. He confidently smirks, carefully calculating a response in his head.

"Why look, it's a peasant boy. Let's all listen to the boy who hath such wisdom and smarts to be standing amongst the mob and not up here on stage," Ryan asserts his snobbish wealth, raising his head proudly into the sky.

"That's right. And because I am a peasant, doth that make me inferior to you?! Am I not a human being?" Jacob uses class warfare to his advantage.

The mob grumbles, their minds becoming infected with Jacob's language of equality. His passion is compelling and the people start to turn on Ryan, becoming suspicious of his intentions.

Ryan obnoxiously chuckles, deflecting Jacob's truisms with a laugh or two.

"We are all but mortal men, young peasant boy. We all have our limitations. Some of us, however, do not know how to survive within those circumstances. Would you help all these people by giving them bread from your farm?! Oh, no, that couldn't be you, because you have no farm! Well, perhaps you could spare a dollar or two to these fine hungry people who need to feed their families? Oh, no, that couldn't be you either. You have no money!"

The crowd again turns, this time in Ryan's direction. Ryan understands their pain and suffering in a realistic manner. They all want equality, but food for their children outweighs freedom and free-thinking any day.

Jacob simmers, just staring down the egotistical giant of a man.

"Your name is Jacob, is it not?" Ryan knows this thorn of a boy all too well.

"It is, Ryan of the North. And we share the same blood!" Jacob drops a bombshell on the crowd and on this arrogant man before him.

The accusation races through the crowd like wildfire, everyone's attention now turned to this newfound gossip, this new dirt.

"Ha! I doubt that!" Ryan again laughs off what Jacob has to say, giving the boy just one of his ears, if that.

"We share the same mother; Margaret of Grench!" Jacob proudly pronounces his heritage.

The mob turns to Ryan for his response over this new slate of evidence.

"Maybe, maybe not. But it is the father that truly counts. And my father and yours are far different from one another. Poor boy, you don't even have a father. You have no last name to speak of. You have no land. Therefore, you have no say!" Ryan shuts down any and all logical options for Jacob to possibly turn the mob back into his favor. He dodges Jacob's attempts to relate them.

The people respect Ryan, he is of a culture they can only dream of. Jacob is one of them, seen as a dreamer, an idealist with the best of intentions. But on cold nights, Jacob will not keep their families warm with blankets. He cannot provide them with necessary shelter.

"You are not a true man," Jacob slanders the aristocrat, a crime in this town.

The people are amazed by the insult. A peasant standing up so sternly to a man of wealth and good name—this is a first for all to see.

"You show me no respect, boy. I am a reasonable man, so once, I shall let it go. But next time I will teach you a lesson."

A couple of guards drag Jacob off by his arms.

"Do not be deceived! The devil appears in many forms!" Jacob shouts his last words to the mob, hoping he made an impact on their frail weak minds.

"So folks, we must band together, friend and foe, peasant and aristocracy, if we are to save and lead our youth into the next century!" Ryan preaches to the crowd, his words trickling off his tongue like butter. And like a sweet frosted desert, the crowd eats up every last bit.

Jacob is sitting alone in a cold, dirty, jail cell. He is dejected, feeling his goal hath run short. He wanted so badly to inspire the people, to give them something they never knew they had inside of them.

"Hello, Jacob." Her soft angelic voice haunts him not only in his dreams, but in reality now, too. Jacob lifts up and his spirits rise upon seeing Claire on the other side of the iron bars.

"Hello, Just Claire." Jacob jumps up to his feet to meet the fair maiden bar-to-bar. "What are you doing in this neighborhood?" Jacob asks sarcastically.

"I should be asking you that. I thought you saved us from the law, not broke it," Claire punches back with a bit of wit herself.

"If you ask me, I think it to be a conspiracy." A quirky smile and precious sparkle of his eyes enchant even the enchanting. Claire and Jacob's eyes become a mirror of one another. They see each other for who they truly are, no indifference to why. Claire turns to the guard and a mere nod from her head gets him quickly to his feet. He rushes to the cell and releases Jacob.

"You saved me." Jacob smiles romantically.

"No, you saved me." Claire displays the inspiration Jacob has given her. Jacob and Claire walk up to the top of the Great Hills overlooking the town. They are seated amongst the beautiful lush green grass. The grass is so full and soft it acts as a comforting mattress. The two heroes are sitting on air as they gaze at one another.

"Who are you?" Jacob asks.

"Remember? I'm Just Claire," she retorts playfully.

"I think you're an angel. You're absolutely enchanting." Claire blushes. "Are you with someone?"

"I am," her response lacks the vigor of a successful relationship.

"Would you be willing to consider another?" Jacob pries, attempting to sneak his way into her front door.

"I might." Claire, deadly serious, penetrates Jacob's eyes with beams of truth and hope. "But now, now I must go back into town."

"I'll walk you," Jacob declares, always displaying his chivalrous intentions. Jacob and Claire walk side by side, laughing, enjoying their final moments together. They are at the brink of town, their budding romance seemingly ready to explode, but for now, they must separate for who knows how long. They turn to one another, preparing for a sad goodbye, both hopeful of an optimistic future.

"So, you've come back again, *brother*." Ryan's words are soaked with sarcasm and negativity. He stands, frowning as his girlfriend consorts with this annoying peasant. Standing behind Ryan is a large group of his supporters, many members of the town mob.

"Back? I never left." Jacob steps forward, exuding his inner strength and confidence. Jacob's words act as the final gauntlet, infuriating Ryan. The aristocratic, smooth-talking politician whips out his sword, readying for a fight.

"Put it away, Ryan." Claire steps forward in-between the two passionately driven men.

"Why, my fair Claire, you wouldn't be wronging me now, would you?"

Jacob snaps his head to look at Claire, in shock over this revealed facts. How could this angel, this beautiful creature, be in love with such a despicable slime ball?

"Him?" A stunned Jacob shows the anguish of this news in his crinkled face, begging for it to be untrue.

"Yes," Claire feels almost guilty about admitting the truth.

"I told you, boy, next time you got in my way, I was going to teach you a lesson," Ryan declares, playing not only to his girlfriend, but to the crowd around. The men standing behind Ryan, mainly the local guards and militia, pull out their swords in support of their leader.

"No!" Ryan orders the men. "He's all mine," he says, with a villainous stare sent Jacob's way in hope of striking fear into the heart of the young boy.

Jacob is no boy and steps up as the heroic man he knows lies inside himself. He gently sets Claire off to the side and takes out his sword, Jacob now turning his focus to the battle before him.

"Please don't do this," Claire begs, not wanting to see the two men fight. "I promise you, my sword will not draw a drop of blood," Jacob pledges, so only Claire can hear.

"Peasant boy!" Ryan orders, as if Jacob is his property. "Peasant—who do you think you are?"

"My name is Jacob." The younger man's head is raised honorably up into the air.

Jacob and Ryan approach one another. Ryan holds his sword out in front of him, whirling it around as if he knows something Jacob does not. He presents a confident, cocky smile, the crowd around them growing and encircling the two warriors. The two men themselves circle one another, remaining about ten feet apart at all times.

"Well...*Jacob,* if you push me, will I not push you?" Ryan again plays to his audience, posing the isolated question to the many people surrounding him.

"Perhaps," Jacob says, confused by Ryan's continued politicking.

"If you knock me down, will I not strike back?" Ryan's intent has now becomes clear. He is stalling, continuing to gain support from the crowd surrounding him. And like putty in his hands, the crowd roars on cue, cheering Ryan on.

"If you wrong me, will I not wrong you?" Ryan points his sword at Jacob, no intention of actually fighting at this moment, still enveloped in his overly dramatic dialogue.

"I hath done no such thing!" Jacob's response is drowned out by the continued roar of the audience.

Ryan grins at Jacob, now having him right where he wants him.

"If you betray me, will I not betray you?" Ryan bellows, sending chills through the onlookers. The mob becomes rowdy, chanting, demanding a fight.

"For this is my testament to you. Let it be heard by all!" Ryan thrusts his sword up into the air and once again the mob rages with excitement. They become blood thirsty, nearly knocking one another over to get a view of the fight.

Ryan and Jacob stop circling around one another like two pacing animals. They seize their movement, now engaging in a contest of deep dark glaring. The hatred is overwhelming. Neither man flinches or blinks. Their faces and postures remain frozen in time.

Suddenly, the crowd roars and cheers are silenced. Ryan's eyes flash down to the ground and then back up to the boy whose head he was prepared to take off. But instead of fight, he's now perplexed, again glancing down at the ground.

Jacob's sword rests on the ground just before his feet. The wind blows just a bit louder, Mother Nature's breath now taking center stage. The mob has taken a back seat and all mouths are dropped open, while all eyes focus on the mysterious young man who stands as a proven hero.

"I will not fight my own blood, whether he admits to it or not. I will not destroy another life over…nothing," Jacob rationalizes.

"BOO! FIGHT! GET ON WITH IT!" Sporadic movement from the crowd in support of a bloody sword fight make their voices heard.

"Pick it up, you fool, or I will kill you where you stand!" Ryan demands under his breath, not wanting to be made a fool of.

"I told you, I will not kill my brother," a solemn Jacob repeats.

Ryan is confused, frustrated, and angry. Some are encouraging him to fight, others in the audience remain as perplexed as he. Slowly but surely the mob comes to an agreement they demand a fight. Their boos grow louder.

Chants of "FAKE!" and "FRAUD!" erupt from the audience.

"There will be no fight today," Jacob turns to the crowd and declares, attempting to defuse their misguided desires.

"FRAUD! FAKE!" The crowd continues their assault, focusing their mob anger on Ryan. They are turning with each second of the stalemate, commanding a fight.

The pressures surrounding Ryan overwhelm him. He squeezes his sword tightly, his head swiveling around at the angry peasants.

Jacob recognizes Ryan's breaking delicate demeanor. Ryan wields his sword around and strikes at Jacob. The younger brighter man is quick to grab his own sword and…CLANK…just fends off the attack. Ryan, a little nervous and uneasy, begins to dance around the circle like a boxer ready to fire a big uppercut. He holds his sword out in front of him, bouncing around. The crowd again joins in the battle, relishing every moment of the action.

Jacob, secure in his abilities, moves very little except to slowly follow Ryan's lead, circling around one another. His feet move swiftly over the dirt, nearly gliding with each step. His eyes are focused on the overly tight grip of his opponent, awaiting them to squeeze even harder. They do. That's when Ryan strikes once again. Jacob is ready, fending off the attack and whipping his sword around, causing Ryan to lose the handle on his weapon. His sword flies out of his hands and falls down to the ground. Jacob is quick to place his steel up against the aristocrat's neck.

The crowd is again silenced, unsure of how to react. The turn of events was again unexpected. Five men, all guards, mere pawns of Ryan, step out with their swords drawn to protect their threatened leader.

Jacob quickly realizes this is a no win proposition. He takes a step back from his opponent, carefully pulling his sword away from the man's lifeline. Then, in an instant, he spins around, chaotically swinging his sword above his head. All the people are scared and confused by this madness. They back away, frightened by the lunacy.

"Ahh!" Jacob roars like a wild animal, his screams echoing in the nearby forest. Everyone gives him room, the women and children running for safety. His screams, his screams pierce the senses, the call to a greater power than any mortal man can bear.

Seventeen

Ryan is sitting comfortably before Doctor Wells, a familiar position for him over the years. The good doctor is seated behind his fine oak desk, as he scans the last of his notes on the young Jacob Crestwood. "I appreciate you coming in, Ryan," Doctor Wells says, opening up the discussion.

"No problem."

"I met with Jacob the other afternoon. We had an interesting discussion."

"I can't remember when I talked to Jake and it wasn't interesting," Ryan responds, a momentary smirk shines through his otherwise drab expression.

"Yes, I know what you mean," Doctor Wells agrees with the confused and obviously frustrated older Crestwood. "I know you've given your all in raising Jacob. Ryan, you've done a masterful job. But listen now to what I have to say."

Ryan leans in, Doctor Wells garnering his complete attention.

"Jacob is exhibiting some behavior that…well, frankly I'm concerned with." Doctor Wells speaks with a serious tone, expressing considerable worry for his young client.

"What do you mean?" Ryan's throat runs dry, nearly too nervous to even ask what might be wrong now.

"A lot of times, a child from a broken home, or in your case, a death in the family, experiences some emotional disorders. With Jacob, things are compounded with you mother who is clinically ill. Being bipolar is one thing. But also suffering from dementia is a difficult one-two punch."

"That's why Jakey comes to see you, Tuesdays," Ryan jumps into the conversation in defense of his younger sibling. "He's a little different, but that's all. Nothing's wrong with him; no disorders or anything. Things are fine at home." Ryan knows that's not to be true, but Jacob is after all, his brother and only family.

"Jacob represses a lot of his feelings and emotions. His dreams are quite traumatic at times. He has some very disturbing feelings toward your father's death. Look, Jacob's a fascinating young man, but socially, he hasn't had the opportunity to develop the proper social skills that are normal for a young man his age. He really only talks with Billy, and to be frank, we both know Billy himself suffers from social disorders." Doctor Wells technically lays out for the laymen Ryan the best he can.

"Doc, Billy's got a lot of issues. He barely talks," Ryan candidly states, trying to separate Jacob from the label of being mentally ill.

"He's very eccentric; much in the way Jacob is. Billy's harmless. Jacob displays certain behavioral patterns that could lead to some outbursts."

Ryan stares at Doctor Wells with a blank expression on his face, understanding very little of what the doctor is saying. He doesn't want to hear it.

"Jacob's like a dam right now." Doctor Wells begins to explain Jacob's predicament in terms Ryan will understand and hopefully hear. "A dam can only hold so much water before it needs to let a little out. But when the force and weight of the water becomes too great for a dam, it's going to eventually burst, and crumble into pieces," Doctor Wells wants to make sure Ryan understands the possible severity of the situation.

"What, you think he's gonna explode or somethin'? Jacob's not aggressive like that." Again Ryan remains stubborn, not wanting to face the truth.

"I've briefed a colleague of mine, Doctor Schwartz, who specializes in child psychology to speak with Jacob. I think it's best to take Jake and place him in a monitored environment so Doctor Schwartz can take a good close look at him."

"Monitor? You mean like my mom? Doctor Wells!" Ryan shakes his head, adamantly objecting to Doctor Wells's suggestion.

"Easy, Ryan. It'll probably just be for a week." Doctor Wells tries to calm Ryan down and reason with him.

"No way, no how! I'm not subjecting Jake to a nuthouse with all them loonies. That's the same as telling him he's crazy himself, and that's not fair. Doc, there's already one Crestwood locked up in here. Isn't that enough?" Ryan returns with his own reasoning, fighting tooth and nail for Jacob.

"Keep a close eye on him, Ryan. I just want what's best for your brother. And I don't know when and I don't know how, but Jacob, sooner than later, is gonna need to blow off some steam. There are a lot of things he's keeping to himself. Maybe you could talk to him, communicate more at home."

"Yeah…we definitely have our differences," Ryan thinks to himself, knowing it's nearly impossible for him and Jacob to maintain an open line of communication.

"If there's a problem, or you just need to talk, don't hesitate to call." Doctor Wells rises to his feet, extending his hand to Ryan.

Ryan nods, standing as well, thankfully shaking the doctor's hand. Ryan turns and exits the office, now more than ever unsure of how to deal with Jacob.

Doctor Wells regretfully watches Ryan walk away, knowing this family's future is quite uncertain.

The local cemetery provides an odd sense of peace for Ryan. When he's troubled or needs to search deep within himself for answers, he goes there. He goes there, because that is where his father rests.

The clouds are forming overhead. Little sun has poked through this day. Gloom has dominated the sky above, a gray blanket of white covering the majority of the sky. The weather too has cooled. No longer is the afternoon spring sun providing its charitable wealth of warmth. The clouds shield Starktown from her guiding light, denying any smiles to reflect upon her.

The wind gently tosses Ryan's hair up off his head, a gust here, and another there. Deep in thought, he strolls to a familiar spot, weaving through tombstone after tombstone. The cemetery is his on this afternoon.

Ryan reaches his destination—a gray tombstone, nothing special, with William Crestwood's name etched at the top. No dates, just the words, "Loving Father," mark the bland, nearly empty stone. Ryan takes a deep breath, preparing himself for the swell of emotions built up inside, and sits down on the lush green grass next to the headstone.

"Hey, Dad." The words trickle out of his mouth as if he was greeting a tragically ill friend. The wind gusts once again, a subtle response back from the heaven perhaps.

"I'm doing all right. Pretty much the same ol' thing. I did meet a girl though. I really like her. I think she's special. When I stare into her eyes, I get that same feeling you told me you got with Mom when ya first spotted her in high school. That butterfly excited feeling. I think my knees are gonna give when I see this girl. You'd like her I think." Ryan pauses, so much more to say. He's staring out just beyond the headstone, occasionally glancing down at his father's engraved name, always wanting to respectfully make eye contact. "You're probably wondering how Mom's doing. I'm sure she'd visit ya if she could. But I'm sure ya know, she's not so good all the time. Doc Wells thinks she's getting a little better though; but I don't really see it. She's still pretty out there."

Ryan takes a breath, his emotions trying to get the best of him. Ryan is the strong son of a strong man, and uses all his will and strength to swallow those tears back. His father would hardly approve of the leader of the family being soft.

"Jacob's having some problems that I just don't know about. He's getting harder to deal with. I'm not too sure if he's doing it on his own or if the crazy bug's finding him. I don't know what to do with him anymore. Things are hard. They're real hard." Ryan takes a deep breath, again holding back the release his body cries out for. "I wish you were here, Dad." Ryan's voice cracks. "I miss you a lot. I really wish you were here." Ryan's voice trails off as he leans back against his father's final resting place, sadly pondering the past and the troubles he now faces in the present.

Late at night the teen hot spot for kids in Starktown is the mini-mall. Many cars, most of which are beat-up old pickups fill the majority of the available spots. A Starbucks, Bob's Big Boy, a well-lit arcade, a multiplex movie theater complex, and Joe's Yogurt are the major hang-outs in Starktown's limited entertainment offerings.

Billy and Jacob spend a lot of time playing arcade games. No sports games for these two boys. They like old magical games, like Zelda, Dragon Quest and some fighting games. The more mystery and intrigue the better. On this night, the boys have taken a night off from the ultimate challenge to destroy all the evil in the world. Instead, they're teaming up as Ninja Turtles fighting crime with hurling pizza's and happy-go-lucky smiles.

Vinni and Casey enter the arcade looking for entertainment of some kind. A fight perhaps? Maybe a video game or two? Each of them are texting on their cell phones and looking casual in t-shirts and jeans. But upon seeing Billy and Jacob working their video game magic,

Vinni's eyes light up like a lion that just spotted wounded prey. Vinni nudges Casey, using a head bob to point his friend's visual direction at the two sitting ducks before them. They put their phones away and have found their fun for the evening.

"They're just asking for it," Vinni jokes with Casey.

Casey agreeably nods, also finding this their best option for this evening's entertainment.

"I want Crestwood." Vinni claims his next victim, happy to get an opportunity to take a swing at the witty young man.

Jacob, calmly and smoothly playing, his smile the expression of a young man in complete control, is a stark contrast to his smaller weaker friend Billy, who's bobbing up and down, using all kinds of body language and struggling from his head down to his toes with the game. Billy's anguish is amusing to Jacob who glances at his little friend, enjoying his extraordinary effort. "Easy, Bill," Jacob jokes.

Billy thrusts back with his body and feet, as if attempting to avoid danger in his game. Upon stepping back, Billy realizes he's jumped on the foot of a stranger.

"Sorry," Billy says as he turns to see who he's stepped on.

Vinni Casterelli and Casey Howard are standing toe to toe with Billy, each sporting a black-hearted smirk. Their evil intentions are expressed with their Joker-like grins, causing Billy to back up in fear of bodily harm.

"Sorry? You stepped on my foot you little runt!" Vinni attempts to intimidate Billy even further.

Upon hearing the sadistic voice of the little Italian with a chip on his shoulder, Jacob snaps his head around, fully aware the situation could get ugly.

"Look, now the other freak wants some," Casey asserts his authority over the situation directing his sadistic comment at Jacob.

"Casey Howard, I talked to Jane Fossey the other day. She said your breath smelled like a dead carp when she kissed you. First base was the only base you reached with her. Now everyone knows." Jacob's words are rambled off his tongue as if he were the bully.

Billy helplessly stares up at his best friend in shock over his verbal assault on the much bigger and tougher duo standing before them. Billy's heart races, wondering what in the world Jacob is up to.

Casey steps forward, angered by Jacob's insults. But Vinni puts his hand up in front of Casey, holding his back.

"Such strong words, Crestwood. Oh, by the way, how's the mom? She still think she's Cleopatra this week? Or is it Elvis?" Vinni and Casey chuckle, amused by their twisted sense of humor.

"That's pretty funny, Vinni. Not quite as funny as your mom having relations with Dale the plumber though. That must have been an awkward day in your house when your dad found out. He just take it?" Jacob attacks, again drawing criticism from Billy's desperate and scared eyes.

Vinni and Casey stop laughing, Vinni now enraged by Jacob's quick wit.

"News travels fast in a small town." Jacob's eyes and words fire like daggers at the heart of Vinni's personal life.

"Come on, Vinni. There's two of us and only one-and-a-half of them," Casey says

"Sorry, boys, we're lovers, not fighters," Jacob replies with a condescending smirk.

"Yeah," Billy says, taking a page from his fearless friend, jabbing back at the two bullies.

Casey grunts, frightening Billy, causing him to jump back, removing any and all bravery in one single noise.

Jacob and Billy march proudly out of the arcade, leaving Vinni and Casey in a state of shock by this sudden bout of fearlessness displayed before them.

But Jacob and Billy are not alone as they exit outside the arcade into the parking lot of the mini-mall. They are being followed by Vinni and Casey, both of whom are smiling, licking their chops.

Billy nervously glances over his shoulder, seeing the two bullies trailing behind each one of his nervous strides. "They're following us, Jake. They're following us." Billy's voice cracks, trying to convey the information to Jacob's ears.

Jacob takes a deep, frustrated breath, growing tired of the situation. He's had enough and abruptly turns around, facing up the two bullies.

"You know what? I think the years of torment you boys generously bestowed upon us in middle school was enough. We don't need to fight you guys to prove—" Jacob's rant is met by a right cross from Casey that comes out of nowhere. Jacob is knocked to the ground, momentarily shaken.

"That's what you get, loud-mouth!" Casey stands over Jacob, his finger flashing down at him, asserting himself as the boss.

"That was supposed to be my punch." Vinni sarcastically smacks Casey's arm.

"Sorry, bro," Casey apologetically replies.

"Hey!" Billy shouts out in defense of his friend.

Billy takes a step toward Jacob and is then forcefully shoved back by the obnoxious Vinni.

"What are you going to do you little freak? Go ahead, tell me what you're going to do!" Vinni begs Billy to step into his world of pain.

Billy is left helpless, unable to do a thing. He stands in place, looking as if he might cry.

"What are you going to do, baby? Are you going to cry?" Again Vinni reaches out with his long arms and knocks Billy backwards. This time the force from the push knocks him onto his back. Billy stays on the ground holding his chest in pain.

A small group of onlookers, mainly high school and junior high locals, have now surrounded the small brouhaha.

Cara also is present amongst the sea of on-lookers. She steps forward curiously to see what is taking place. Cara sees Billy on the ground and gets upset, rushing over to help him up.

"Look, they got a freak girl to help them up! Ha-ha!" Casey blurts out, both Vinni and Casey thoroughly amused.

Jacob, blood trickling out of the side of his mouth, turns from a look of shock over being struck in the face to boiling rage in a manner he's never felt before. Jacob leaves the blood on the side of his mouth untouched, wanting everyone to view it as a badge of courage. He looks over and sees Billy helped up by Cara and knows what he must do. He looks to his hand and sees a sword glimmering in the moonlight. He rises to his feet, shocking everyone.

Billy stares in awe of his friend, having never seen such bravery and stupidity from Jacob. He sees a look from Jacob he has never seen before.

Jacob stares angrily at Casey, his eyes attempting to pierce the soul of his foe.

"Oh, hey, lookie here, big-mouth wants some more." The loathsome Casey directs everyone's attention to his next and final victorious blow.

"Jake-don't," Cara says, standing next to Billy, a warning from one outcast to another.

Jacob is in a zone. He cares little about the noise heard around him.

Casey steps forward to again pop Jacob but this time, his fist doesn't connect. In fact, as Casey brings his arm back, his hands clinched tight ready to strike Jacob, a curious feeling overcomes the bully. It's a feeling unlike any other he's ever experienced. Casey is knocked to the ground, completely unconscious, blood spilling out of his mouth. One, maybe two teeth have been knocked out, and standing over the flattened bully is Jacob, his fist bloodied from the blow, a rabid hunger projected down at his prey. Jacob looks at his hand and sees the shimmering sword glowing in the dark night.

Absolute silence has overcome the scene of the fight. No one is cheering for more, or applauding any great victory. The shocking view has silenced everyone's tongues.

Vinni, put in an unfamiliar position himself, his best friend and partner in crime laid out on the ground before him, hesitates, thinking about what to do. Then his animalistic instincts take over and he lunges at Jacob with his clinched fist.

"Jacob!" yells Billy, attempting to protect his back the best he can.

Jacob instinctively ducks, Vinni's wild right missing badly.

"Oh, much too slow. Try again, you over-sized ox!" Jacob now plays to the crowd, the kids around applauding and rooting their new hero to victory.

Vinni takes another wild swing, this time with his left. Jacob bobs and weaves like Muhammed Ali, easily avoiding the reckless punches.

"Looks like we have a major winner here, kids! Let's all give the dope a hand for trying!" Jacob, animated and confident, strolls around the now well-defined circle of lookieloos. The crowd chants, applauds, and laughs, having the time of their lives. Jacob's invincibility races through their excited hearts, and they cheer for him as if he were fighting for all the underdogs everywhere. Jacob sees himself wielding around his sword, entertaining the onlookers. Vinni chases Jacob around the circle and chaotically lunges after him with another futile punch. But this time, Jacob counters Vinni's misfire with a strike of his own. Jacob knocks Vinni flush in the mouth, the giant of a young man crumbling like a sack of potatoes down to the ground.

The crowd roars with excitement, wanting Jacob to finish the thug off. Jacob appeases the crowd, pouncing on Vinni to administer the final blows.

"The gauntlet hath been thrown down! And who is the victor I ask you? Who is the victor?!" Jacob shouts out in a dramatically charged outburst.

Billy watches his possessed friend, unsure of what has become of him. The crowd wants more, but Billy just wants things to end.

Jacob pummels the bully, a left, then a right. Again and again, he hits Vinni.

"Answer me! Answer me!" Jacob shouts to the unconscious bully, demanding retribution for a history plagued with the thug's brutality.

"Jacob! Jacob!" Billy and Cara rush over to Jacob, his face now getting splattered with the other boy's blood. They pull Jacob back, the two boys and girl falling back down to the ground. Blood has spilled all over the cement boxing surface. The two town bullies lay unconscious on the ground, their wits completely knocked out of them. The crowd isn't asking for more. They're staring at Jacob wondering what blood-thirsty animal had been awakened inside, and if that animal would attack them.

"It's okay. It's okay." Billy tries to calm Jacob down, holding his arms around him.

"You okay, Jake?" Cara asks with concern.

Jacob's breathing begins to slow, his deep charged breaths lessening as the seconds go by. He rolls away from Billy onto his side.

"Take it easy. It's okay," Billy continues to try and calm his friend, hoping he exorcised the demons awakened inside.

Jacob looks to his hand and his sword is gone. He looks to the ground and sees the bloodied bully at his feet, knocked unconscious.

"I'm sorry. I'm so sorry," Jacob authentically apologizes, realizing he is wrong.

Crack! Suddenly, Jacob is struck over the top of the head by a glass bottle courtesy of a bloodied Casey who finally came to.

"Hey!" A uniformed officer comes rushing through the crowd and into the circle. The officer stares at the three boys and the great deal of blood spilt in this war.

"My God!" The officer stares at the scene in shock, the extent of the violence far greater than any lesser tussles more familiar to the teens of Starktown.

Sheriff Bartlet is standing beside the nurse's station when Ryan comes rushing into the hospital. The sheriff is a good, honest man. He's lived all his life in the confines of Starktown and has maintained a good demeanor with all the citizens in town. He's a townie of fifty-five years and knows the Crestwoods quite well. Sheriff Bartlet and Jess Crestwood used to go hunting back in the day. His hair has thinned and gone somewhat gray, his belly has grown large and his face has become wrinkled. One thing is for sure, good old Sheriff Bartlet always tells it like it is.

"Sheriff, what happened?" Ryan asks nervously.

"He's fine. He got into it with Casterelli and the Howard boy." The sheriff speaks with a slight easy-going southern drawl.

"Can I take him home?" Ryan wants to get Jacob away from any unlawful scrutiny quickly.

"Doc wants him to stay the night, Ryan. I think it's best that way. Let the boy ease things off."

"Okay. I guess that'll be fine, if that's what the doctor wants." Ryan appears nervous, a little edgy.

"Ya know, Jacob gave the Casterelli boy a good shiner, one the likes that kid ain't ever seen," Bartlet chuckles, almost relieved somebody finally gave a little back to the little terror.

"Really?" Ryan is surprised and impressed by the news, unsure of what to say.

"That's nothing though. His big buddy, Casey Howard…whew! Jacob knocked that one senseless! Just between you and me, he kicked the livin' crud out of those boys. And I'm kinda glad." Bartlet smiles and pats Ryan on the back.

"Are there going to be any…" Ryan hints towards actions taken by the law.

"Nah! No charges. This one will just go down as a minor incident for Jake. The other boys have a long history though. They'll have to do some service to make amends for their behavior. Add some time to their group therapy. But, in all seriousness Ryan, Jacob is sixteen. Almost a man. He can't get caught up in any brawls. If it happens again, he'll have to pay the penalty." Sheriff Bartlet, as he always does, lay the situation out before Ryan honestly.

"Thanks, Sheriff. I'm sure it was a one-time thing."

"These kids go to school with Jake?" Ryan curiously asks.

"Oh, yeah. Probably terrorize him awful like a lot of kids there." Sheriff Bartlet is well-versed on the history of Casterelli and Howard.

"I guess it's a good thing they're on summer break then," Ryan thinks to himself.

"Oh, definitely. Good for us all," Bartlet ominously points out diffusing the possibility of any retaliation for Jacob and Billy. "Those two have bothered Jacob and Billy a lot. Pushed them around quite a bit. Bullies to their core, those two are."

"Jake never told me about those two kids," Ryan thinks to himself.

"Yeah. They're a handful."

"It will be just a one-time thing though. I'll talk to Jakey," Ryan assures Bartlet again.

"I figured such. Have a good one, Ryan. Say hi to your mom for me," Bartlet heads towards the exit, his job done.

"Thank you, Sheriff." Ryan thinks deeply about what to do with Jacob, another unforeseen pothole in life struck dead on.

Jacob is lying in his hospital room, fast asleep. A head dressing is wrapped around his forehead much like a headband, with another bandage just above his temple covering the wound he suffered from the bottle.

Ryan, standing at the doorway to the room, runs his hands over his face, frustrated and tired. He drags himself over to a cushioned guest chair and quietly carries it over to the bed just beside his little brother. Ryan sits himself down and prepares himself to spend the night in the chair, adjusting his posture, trying to get as comfortable as possible.

Eighteen

This Saturday morning has been one of the gloomiest days in weeks. The clouds have solidified their positioning in the sky and are dousing any and all hopes of the sun making an appearance. For the fourth day in a row, the temperature has dropped. Today, it's not expected to get any warmer than fifty degrees. Mother Nature is painting an ominous picture for Starktown.

On the upside though, the partially built Flowers home is looking almost homey. Insulation is being added all throughout the interior of the walls with the water heater soon to follow.

Ryan, his hair a mess and with dark rings under his eyes, jumps out of his pickup truck, rushing around to the work site.

Martin and Carlos are chilling outside the house drinking from two steaming hot Styrofoam cups of coffee.

"What's up, boss?" Carlos welcomes the exhausted Ryan as he drags himself over to his work team.

"Hey, 'Los," Ryan groggily returns.

"Man, I hate working on Saturdays," Martin whines.

"We gotta catch up, man. I hate it too, but we gotta finish the job on time," Ryan preaches to his team, attempting to provide a small tidbit of motivation.

Carlos and Martin remain unmotivated, both tired themselves, sipping their coffee.

"Where's Stan?" Ryan asks curiously, looking around, confused over his whereabouts.

"Yeah, where is that freak?" Martin now recognizes his non-presence.

"Stan couldn't find his rear end, what surprises you about him not being here on a Saturday?" Carlos jokes.

Carlos and Martin chuckle, Stan the butt of their jokes even though he's nowhere to be seen.

"Hey!" Ryan hollers sternly, putting an end to the laughter. "I'm sure Stan could find his butt if he really needed to! It just might take a day or two," Ryan surprises them, initiating an outburst of laughter. The three men laugh, undercutting their weekend work frustrations.

Claire's BMW is parked out front of the Crestwood home. The wind is now picking up, gusts of ten and fifteen mile per hour cause leaves to carry across the yards and streets in the neighborhood.

The doorbell rings throughout the old two-story home. Jacob opens up the front door, his lip cut, a bandage taped to the side of his forehead, and a bruise on his cheek. Equally eye-catching is the oversized bright orange foam cowboy hat resting on top of his head, shadowing the numerous blemishes on and around his face. A black martial arts robe is draped over Jacob's entire body, and rubber orange rain boots match the outlandish hat worn on top of his head.

Claire immediately spots the bruises and a look of concern overcomes her.

"Oh, my gosh! What happened to your face?" Claire reaches out with her gentle soft fingers and touches the bruises here and there on Jacob's face.

"I took a bad fall." Jacob plays the bruises down, trying to make them sound mysterious.

"I love the outfit," Claire accepts Jacob's obviously vague response and lightens up the subject matter.

"I made it up myself," Jacob replies with a quirky smile. Jacob steps aside, respectfully holding his arm out and bowing, inviting Claire to enter his home.

"I'm sure," Claire giggles as she passes by Jacob on her way into the house.

"Are you ready to bake or what?" Jacob asks, with a whirl of excitement as he shuts the front door.

"You betcha!" Claire returns with some exuberance of her own.

"Awesome!" Jacob rushes in front of Claire, leading her towards the kitchen.

"Where's Ryan?" Claire looks around curiously, seeing no signs of the elder Crestwood. Claire stops in the dining room.

"That workaholic!" Jacob's response is of no surprise to him, but tries to play off his brother as something he's not. "That guy will work until dawn unless you tell him he has to sleep at nights. I think he said he'd be home in a couple of hours," Jacob continues to embellish.

"Oh," Claire is a little surprised and disappointed over Ryan's lack of presence.

"He wanted us to start without him. Come on." Again Jacob urges Claire to follow him into the kitchen.

The kitchen has been transformed into a viewing room of Jacob's lifelong works. Poems and stories are attached to any and everything in the kitchen. Tables, the walls, the ceiling—everywhere there could be a piece of paper, there is. Hundreds and hundreds of pages of writing fill the kitchen. Some pieces are very short, while others fill the full capacity of their page.

Claire slowly turns around looking at all the pages of writing in awe of their strategic placement and their overwhelming abundance.

"So now you can read while we bake," Jacob rationalizes to the big city girl.

"My God," Claire continues her look of astonishment. She tilts her head back and sees a ceiling filled with work. She shakes her head.

"What are they doing up there?" Claire asks with her necked cranked back, staring up at the many pages up on the ceiling.

"In case you decided to lie down and take a break." Jacob lies on the ground as an example of what he means.

"See, you could just read." Jacob looks up at his ceiling, continuing to display his point.

"I'm not sure if I'll be able to read it from all the way down there," Claire grins, doubting Jacob's presentation. Jacob, as if expecting Claire's response, lights up, acting as if he has all the answers.

"I know! That's why I got these," Jacob grabs a pair of binoculars he had specially placed on one of the kitchen chairs.

"You thought of everything, didn't you?" Claire smiles at Jacob, her eyes sparkling like the angel she is.

Jacob loses all his thoughts, his mind cleared and halted by the twinkling eyes of the adorable creature standing before him. Claire turns away, breaking Jacob's trance. He regains his senses, remembering the tasks at hand.

"Oh, I...I got an outfit for you, too." Jacob looks around, attempting to remember the placement of this special cookware he has put aside for the beautiful woman.

"For me?" Claire is surprised and a little afraid of what concoction Jacob has in store for her.

"Of course, all chefs must have chef attire," Jacob points out intelligently.

"Did you learn that on the Food Channel too?" Claire reaches back in her memory bank for the pun.

"No, on David Letterman. Wolfman Jack came on—" Jacob begins his explanation.

"I think you mean Wolfgang Puck," Claire interrupts, correcting Jacob, but at the same time, amused by his innocent mistake.

"I know it was some kind of wolf, but he expressed the importance of...wait a second, maybe it wasn't you looking good, maybe it was the food looking good. I don't know. It was something about looking good."

"Oh!" Jacob says, remembering just where he left Claire's outfit. He opens up the cabinet below the sink and pulls out a large cylindrical chef's hat and a rainbow colored apron. He proudly offers them to Claire.

Claire looks the outfit over, a hesitant smirk on her face.

"This will be your armor." Jacob speaks to her as if she had been just knighted.

"My armor?" Claire accepts the odd clothing.

"But of course, your armor! We wouldn't want any bits of egg or flour ruining your beautiful clothing."

Jacob elicits a flattered smile from Claire, and turns his back to her, letting out a relieved and nervous breath of air. He knows this may be his only chance to get the angel who so suddenly swooped into his world on a cloud and just as easily may be taken away. He grabs a box of cake mix and turns back around.

Claire poses, dressed in Jacob's ridiculous ensemble, oddly enjoying herself. She flails her arms, smiling ear to ear. Her look momentarily captivates Jacob, rendering the impetuous boy speechless.

"Nice," Jacob compliments, finally. Again he gathers his senses together, holding the cake mix up in the air, almost as a shield of armor for his heart.
"Unfortunately…Wolf, whatever his name, didn't have his own cake mix. But I was lucky enough to find Betty Crocker. I hear she's an excellent cook. So, here."

Claire gladly accepts the box of cake mix, ready to do her part. Claire flips the box around and examines its back, surveying for the instructions.

Meanwhile, Jacob pulls out a pan and sets it down on the counter next to some of the cake ingredients. Jacob then grabs an unopened bag of flour already set upon the counter. Jacob tries to tear the bag, but his fingers aren't strong enough.

"First we need to put a touch of flour on the pan." Jacob continues struggling with the bag, his face contorting, every muscle in his entire body attempting to rip open this fussy bag.

"Why don't you let me help you with that," Claire says, almost motherly, tender. She sets her box of cake mix down on the counter and steps up next to Jacob, offering her services.

"I can do it," Jacob gasps out loud, his teeth grinding.

"It's going to go everywhere if you open it. Why don't you just use scissors?"

"What, you don't think I'm strong enough?" Jacob takes the challenge upon himself to show his lady how manly and strong he actually is.

"It's not that, it's just…"

Jacob lets out a powerful grunt and the package of flour explodes all over Claire. She has flour on her face, neck, clothes, and pants. She's almost like a spring snow-woman. Jacob looks a shocked and stunned Claire over, trying his hardest to hold his laughter in, nearly busting at the seams.

"I told you I was strong enough," Jacob responds softly, smiling, trying to control himself.

"You're gonna get it now," Claire replies, with a mischievous smirk. Claire grabs a handful of flour and chases after Jacob, the two circling one another around the kitchen table. The two of them giggle, having a wonderfully immature time. Jacob dashes off out of the kitchen and Claire follows, the chase continuing.

Nana is resting comfortably in her living room, gently rocking back and forth. Her hands are knitting and weaving, creating yet another horrendous plaid scarf for Billy to toss onto the floor of his closet.

Billy comes jogging into the living room, all decked out in his fishing garb. He's got a camouflage circular brimmed fishing hat, a matching vest, and sweat pants. He's ready to battle the muddy trenches of Lake Maya with his black rubber rain boots.

"Nana, I'm meeting Jacob at the lake," Billy says.

"Just be home before sundown." Nana passes off the parental directions without even a glance.

"Okay, I'm gonna go grab my stuff," Billy says, happily accepting Nana's terms as he does all the time.

"All right, dear," she says, focusing all her attention on her knitting.

Billy notices Nana preoccupied with her soothing afternoon activities and quietly slips into the hallway. Billy climbs into the basement, softly setting the trap door closed. He eases his way down the hanging ladder and enthusiastically rushes over to his stash of nudie magazines. He grabs a few and hurries back over to the hanging ladder. He tries to remain as quiet as possible, climbing up the creaking wood steps. He struggles with just one arm to hold on, the other occupied with the many pages of eye candy grasped close to Billy's adolescent body.

He reaches up to the door, attempting to push it open. The metal latch has jammed the door shut and Billy's one arm isn't nearly strong enough to shove it open. He pushes and pushes with his one free hand, but to no avail, the door not budging an inch. Billy reaches up onto his tiptoes, trying to get every ounce of force he can muster into his one right hand. Billy's right foot slips off the narrow wood step and he immediately loses his balance, falling off the ladder and down to the ground. His back and then his head strike the ground hard, Billy's eyes closing, unconscious. He lay sprawled out on the ground, his dirty magazines strewn across the basement floor. A small trickle of blood flows out from underneath Billy's unconscious head.

Meanwhile, upstairs in the living room, Nana listens for any other noises. The wind whips up outside and tosses leaves and sticks all about, the tress rustling around as if they had been shaken. Nana again turns her attentions to her knitting, the afternoon hours racing by.

———

    A blizzard has blown through the Crestwood kitchen, leaving in its wake a thick coating of white flour. The entire kitchen floor, as well as its counters, have been doused in the white powder.

    "Just a little bit more," Jacob, covered head to toe in flour, instructs himself, as he finishes pouring the cake batter out of its bowl and into the tin pan.

    Claire, also blanketed like a bad snow day in the winter, is standing in front of the wall reading one of many poems and stories.

    "This about does it," Jacob satisfied, sets the bowl down and looks over his batter filled tin pan.

    "These are all great! You ever think about trying to publish them or entering any writing contests?" Claire asks, continuing to survey the wall.

    "Publish? I wouldn't know where to go to do that kind of stuff. I just write stuff that's on my mind and in my heart. I never even thought anyone but me would ever see these. You're the only other person that's read them."

    "Ryan hasn't even read these?" Claire's in disbelief.

    "Nope," Jacob states casually. "And anyway, what if other people don't like them? What if they hate them?"

    "You don't strike me as the type of person that worries about what other people think of you."

    "It's not me that people usually see. The words on these papers are me. They represent all that is me. Everything else is just window dressing."

    "You're not an easy one to figure, Jacob Crestwood."

    Jacob catches Claire's eyes and for a moment, their silence means volumes to him. He breathes when she breathes. He blinks when she blinks. Claire's eyes break Jacob's trance as she focuses on the batter filled tin pan.

"Oh, yes," Jacob steps out of his hypnotic state. "You need to set the oven at three hundred and seventy-five degrees."

Claire nods and turns to the oven, looking over the various foreign buttons. She adjusts them accordingly.

"Ready, captain," Claire role-plays with Jacob.

"Well…what are you waiting for? Open the bomb bay doors!" Jacob shouts out his order, adhering strictly to the captain's code.

"Bomb bay doors? Oh!" Claire thinks and realizes what Jacob's talking about. She opens the oven door, the recently lit up gas machine coughing out a warm breath of air. Jacob takes the tin of cake mix and slides it into the artillery chamber.

"Close bomb bay doors!" Jacob barks out another order.

"Bomb bay doors closing!" Claire repeats and carries out her superior officer's command. "Bomb bay doors are closed," Claire smiles, her task completed.

Jacob takes out a timer and sets it at fifty minutes. He starts it and the ticking begins.

"We have fifty minutes to save the world. What do you suggest we do?" Jacob turns seriously to Claire, posing his life-threatening question to her.

"How about we go for a drive?" Claire offers up, with a little dramatic flair.

"Excellent idea," Jacob smiles, luke-warm to the idea.

Ryan, exhausted, his shirt and face dirtied from a hard day's work, drags his tired body over to Martin who's sitting on a crate, drinking a beer. He too is dirtied and sweaty from a long Saturday of construction.

"I need your cell phone," Ryan yawns, tired not only from the day's labor, but from last night's trying escapade.

"Why?" Martin twinges with agitation. He's away from his soft tired old ripped recliner, a friend that regularly welcomes Martin with open arms on the weekend.

"I have to make a call," Ryan matches Martin's foul mood with one of his own.

"You're calling Claire, aren't you?" A smile overcomes Martin, sensing an opportunity to make fun of his good friend.

"If you must know, I gotta call home."

"Right," Martin, nodding and smiling, not believing Ryan for a second. "Come on, already! Look, I'll give you a dollar for the call!" Martin reluctantly pulls out his cell phone and hands it to Ryan.

"Thank you," a relieved Ryan quickly begins dialing.

"You better be calling your house. If my wife sees some strange number on the bill, I'll be living in couch city!" Martin again complains.

"Don't worry!" Ryan grumbles in return.

The telephones ring inside the Crestwood home. The living room and Ryan's bedroom remain silent and empty, no one rushing to answer a phone.

Ryan impatiently taps his feet, waiting for someone who isn't there to answer the call. Ryan's restlessness leads him to pace back and forth, waiting and waiting while the phone rings and rings.

"Where can they be?" Ryan asks, confused and annoyed by the vacant line of the other end of the telephone.

Claire's BMW goes zooming down Thompson Road. Jacob is standing tall in the car, free as a bird, the wind striking his face. He's leaning on the dash, the convertible top retracted down behind the back seat of the luxury vehicle.

Claire nervously glances over at him, worried by Jacob's willingness to stand freely in the cross wind.

"Okay-okay! Sit down! You're making me nervous," Claire says tremulously to Jacob, her voice fighting the force of the wind barreling down upon them.

"Never!" Jacob shouts, his eyes closed, enjoying the absolute thrill of flight. The chilled air invigorates Jacob's senses, fulfilling nearly all his veiled desires.

Claire drives cautiously, glancing back and forth at Jacob, now becoming more and more curious over his stirring experience.

"Is that fun?" Claire asks timidly, gaining a taste for Jacob's adventurous tendencies.

Jacob's eyes fly open in shock. He looks at Claire as if she were an alien and plops himself back down in his seat.

"You've never stood up in this car and felt the wind racing against your face, like you were just…free? Free like a bird soaring through the sky." Jacob's face shows pity and anguish for the grounded woman sitting beside him.

"It's my car. Usually, I'm driving," Claire answers. Inside, however, Jacob has initiated a rarely tapped romantic spirit hidden just below Claire's angelic exterior. "Here, I'll pull over and you can drive," Claire says, now the one exploding with excitement, leaping at the opportunity to soar like a bird.

Claire steers her BMW over to the side of the road and puts it in park. She jumps out of the driver's seat and rushes around to the passenger side of the car. Jacob, however, remains seated silently in the passenger seat, his sense of adventure long gone. He's reverted from the heroic adventurer to a scared, apprehensive child.

"It's okay. I trust you to drive my car."

"It's not that. It's just I...I..."Jacob searches for some macho comeback, but stutters along with nothing coming to mind.

"What is it?" Claire is stumped by Jacob's uncharacteristic silence.

"I don't know how to drive," Jacob admits timidly.

"That's all right, nobody in this world *really* does," Claire jokes.

"No, I really don't know. I've never driven a car in my life. I don't know what these buttons and sticks do. I always ride my bike around town," Jacob explains.

"Well..." Claire thinks. "It's never too late to learn," she optimistically offers up to Jacob.

"Say again?" Jacob asks with the hint of fear in his voice, gulping shortly after.

"You heard me. Get in the driver's seat," Claire orders, taking over control of the ship.

"Now?" All of a sudden Jacob has retracted into a shell like a scared turtle.

"Wait a second. Let me try and understand this. You're scared about trying something different? The great Jacob Crestwood is scared?" Claire dares the young man like kid on the playground.

"Scared?" Jacob laughs at the word, mocking Claire's daring remarks. "I could slay the mightiest of dragons with one hand tied behind my back!" Jacob proclaims, thrusting his finger up into the air.

"Good. Now get in the driver's seat, Sir Lancelot," Claire smiles, waiting for Jacob to slide his rear into the captain's chair.

Jacob takes a deep breath and reluctantly slides over into the driver's seat. Claire happily nods and sits herself down into the passenger's seat. Jacob nervously looks the dashboard of the car over, all the buttons and knobs so foreign to him. The car dash might as well be an airplane cockpit.

"Ya know, this could be very dangerous. We could get hit by a truck or a train or something," Jacob rambles, his voice tweaking just a bit.

Claire looks down either side of the empty road. There isn't a car in sight for as far as the eyes can see.

"I gotta hunch it's gonna be okay."

"Okay." Jacob takes a deep nervous breath, attempting to calm himself down. His eyes pan back and forth around the dash, confused over what to do first. His breathing quickens and panic sets in his mind. What if I crash? What if I kill the two of us? The questions rattle off one after another, clouding Jacob's mind.

"Here," Claire leans over Jacob, shifting the car into drive.

Ever so slowly, the car creeps forward. Almost immediately, Jacob throws his hands up into the air, confused over the car crawling forward inches at a time.

"I'm not doing this!" Jacob shouts, thinking the car may just be demonically possessed.

"It's all right. On your right is the gas and on the left is the brake," Claire points to the pedals beside Jacob's shaky right foot.

"Fear is my friend. Fear is my friend. Fear is my friend," Jacob repeats over and over again in his head, just barely mumbling loud enough for Claire to hear.

"What?" Claire asks, unable to understand the words leaking from Jacob's lips.

"Isn't there some kind of clutch thingie?" Jacob asks Claire, still having trouble finding his way around the car.

"No. No clutch thingies," Claire enlightens the younger, naïve boy.

Jacob abruptly strikes the brake with his right foot, causing the car to come to an uneasy halt. The two passengers' bodies thrust forward and then back against the seats of the car. Jacob and Claire remain silent for a moment, each thinking of what to say. Jacob feels as if he's done something wrong, still utterly confused over the workings of the automobile. Claire ponders words of advice for the virginal driver.

"Think of this car as an unencumbered poem. Your feet will dictate the mood and movement of each verse. It can be fluent or it can be choppy. You decide how the poem flows. Now try," Claire says, hoping these words of advice will guide him better than before.

"Poem…fluent…okay," Jacob repeats to himself, taking Claire's words of advice to heart.

He gently steps on the gas, the car momentarily lunging forward. He then slams on the brakes, frightened by the car's sudden movement, similar to before.

"That was a bit choppy." Claire's body has firmed up, now a little concerned over the welfare of her fairly expensive BMW.

"Tell me about it. But I think I got the hang of this now. I drove a tractor a couple of times. This is kinda similar." With renewed confidence, Jacob prepares himself to launch forward again.

"Okay, if you say so." Claire wants so badly to believe she and her car are safe, but hesitates to believe Jacob at this point.

"Buckle up," Jacob recommends.

Claire quickly buckles herself in, and within a second of her safety belt being fastened, she's thrust back in her seat. Jacob zooms down Thompson Road like a pro.

"Ha!" Jacob erupts with excitement. "I'm doing it, Claire! I'm doing it!" Jacob proclaims victoriously, overwhelmed by the rush of driving.

"Yeah! You really are!" Claire glances over at Jacob repeatedly, keeping one eye on the moving road and the other on the rookie driver. Jacob has no problem maneuvering the car, flying at more than thirty miles per hour down the dirt laced cement road.

"I'm gonna do it!" Claire says, preparing herself to stand up in the car.

"Go for it! I've got a handle on things!" Jacob fancies himself a professional driver, giving Claire the green light to rise up into the wind.

Claire rises carefully, standing up into Mother Nature's cross hairs, the cool wind deflecting off the sides of her rosy cheeks. Claire shoots her arms up into the air, claiming her own victory, a joyous smile accompanying her feeling of complete elation and joy. Claire and Jacob shout, their bodies and souls exploding with rushes of energy and accomplishment.

The BMW zooms down the road, leaving in its wake dust and inhibitions.

The construction crew's day has finally come to a close. Martin carries Ryan's old rusty tool box and tosses it into the floorboard of his front seat.

"Martin!" Ryan calls out, running over to his truck.

"It's on your front seat." For the tenth time today, Martin relinquishes his phone to Ryan to make a call. The cell phone is resting comfortably on the passenger's seat of Ryan's truck.

"Thanks." Ryan snatches up the phone and dials home again.

Once again the phones in the Crestwood household ring, with no one to answer them.

"Argh!" Ryan lets out a thunderous roar of frustration. "What the heck's going on?"

The native violets are just coming into bloom along the crest of the Shawnee overlooking Lake Maya. Amongst the lush grass are thick sporadically placed oak trees. They are the best and only cure for hot Indian summer days.

On this day however, shade is offered by the cold dark clouds dominating the sky above.

Claire strolls over the peak of the hills overlooking Lake Maya, staring down at the picturesque view as if she were looking at a Monet. The world around Lake Maya is breathtaking. The chilled air only adds to the flourishing yet subtle colors which spring offers in the well preserved area. The mighty oaks, the peaceful serene waters of Maya, the strategic splashing of purple amongst the lush green backdrop, the cherry red cardinals and their song of love, all present a portrait of earthly perfection.

"Wow. So this is where you fish?" Claire asks, in awe of the natural world surrounding her.

"Me and Billy. This is where we come," Jacob looks the land over in-taking in her beauty as if seeing her for the first time. Her amazing arms, her powerful body, her soft wavy hairs, and all the children that reside within her protection; Mother Nature offers everything Jacob could ever dream of. Every visit to Maya is his first.

"Let's sit down," Claire suggests, knowing full well she's on Jacob's turf.

"Okay." Jacob continues to enjoy all the Shawnee and Maya have to offer. The two soothed souls take a soft seat atop the Shawnee mattress.

"This is beautiful, Jacob. I mean, it's *really* beautiful," Claire comments wholeheartedly.

"I love this moment. Right now, I think this time is my favorite time." Jacob stares seriously out at the world around them.

"What do you mean?" Claire queries, almost begging for some existential response.

"The smell of rain before even a drop has fallen. The cool chilled air swirling about, the calm of a serene spring day on the brink of near disaster as the hot humid summer creeps in and battles spring for its last breath. The wind will blow, the rain will fall and some of this undeniable beauty will be swept away in the hands of time. But you can't destroy this beauty. Rain, fire, a blizzard or a hurricane, it's survived all that the world has thrown at it. It's even survived man. So tomorrow, after the rain has fallen and the face of the beautiful painting has changed, left in its wake will be the firm memory of what life is truly about. It's the most primal of rules. Life breeds death. But the opposite is true as well. The two work hand in hand. They're as extraordinary as the freshly bloomed fragile violets spread about these grassy knolls. Cool, huh?" Jacob now turns to Claire with a question far less perplexing than the philosophical diatribe he just delivered.

"Yes. It is cool. You're a complex soul, Mr. Crestwood."

"You mind if I ask you a few questions?" Jacob queries.

"No. Go right ahead," Claire offers honestly to Jacob.

"You're new in this town, coming from a much larger city. City life is far different from out here in Starktown.

Why?" Jacob ends with a direct question.

"What do you mean?" Claire smiles, evading a question that she herself has been avoiding for days.

"Well, as I see it, people usually run away from small towns to go to bigger ones. The only people that come here are folks on the lam or somebody that has been seriously wronged in some way. Either way, both parties are on the run," Jacob deducts logically.

Claire smiles, looking down to the ground, but she'll find no help or hiding places down there. Jacob has cornered her, and she lifts her head back up to fight her way out.

"Okay. Before I answer your well-outlined question, let me ask you this: for such an intelligent and creative young guy, it surprises me that you're not doing more with yourself. It seems like you don't really do anything. You don't seem to have any goals. Why?" Claire fires back, successfully boxing Jacob into a corner.

"Touché, Just Claire," Jacob says, giving Claire her due credit for an equally challenging line of questioning. "I can answer that. What you and everyone else call, 'not doing anything' is me enjoying every bit of what life has to offer. I do what I want, what I feel. I have no regrets. There's no big account to win or lose. There's no great stock market rises or drops for me. I live my life enjoying every moment of my time." Jacob rises to his feet, once again looking over the beautiful land. "Look at all we have. No matter how bad things get, you must always remember this beauty. We always have to remember how beautiful the world actually is, even when we're staring into the ugly eyes of destruction or deceit. The world is what guides my words, that which is truest to my heart. It's every beautiful poem, sweet story and romantic song. You can hear Mother Nature's beauty in Vivaldi's *Seasons*. You can hear her sweet breath flowing along in almost every piece of art. She inspires us all. All our hopes and dreams are based on the knowledge we've gained from this extraordinary place. To work in an office every day of your life would be to jail yourself from all this beauty. There can't be those kinds of limitations. Not for me."

"Sometimes you don't have a choice," Claire realistically and poignantly replies.

"You always have choices. It's just some people are too afraid to make them." Jacob's eyes sparkle with this message he has been long waiting to deliver. He stares at Claire; it's now her turn to spill the beans.

"I guess it's my turn." Claire gets her cue to begin her diatribe. "I haven't told this to anybody, so you better not play telephone with this. I had a pretty good job and a pretty nice relationship. Needless to say, they both got bad real fast. I needed to change my environment. I was choking in the big city. I couldn't breathe. The walls of my apartment weren't the right color and the air was too smoggy. There were people everywhere I looked and each one of them was judging me. I needed to breathe. I needed air. My friend had a job for me out here, so I thought I'd give it a shot. I'm not really sure what's next. It's an interesting thing, to know one day exactly where your life is heading, and the next to start all over and not know a single thing."

"As long as you know yourself." Jacob carves out an even deeper plain to this already intense conversation.

"I feel…"

"Stranded," Jacob says, finishing Claire's thought, understanding every bit of what she feels.

"Kind of. You like to analyze people, don't you?" Clair points out insightfully.

"I watch people. That's what I do. I'm a voyeur of all life."

"What do you think of your brother?" Claire changes the subject, but stays inside Jacob's fascinating intellect.

"Ryan, he's cool." Jacob's eyes roll down to the ground again. Claire has hit another soft spot in his life.

"Yeah right!" Claire doesn't buy Jacob's primitive answer for a second. "There's something wedged between you guys. I feel it every time I'm around the two of you."

"If you ask Ryan, he would say it's reality or responsibility. If you ask me, I say it's life." Jacob lays down the two brothers ideals in their simplest forms.

The conversation reaches the bottom of the pool; it can travel no deeper. The two participants remain solemn, each reviewing ideas that have recently been spewed out into the cool air that grows more humid and suffocating by the day.

Jacob picks a freshly bloomed violet, holding it up before his eyes.

"The innocence is lost, but not forgotten," Jacob dramatically begins, rising to his feet.

Claire's eyes follow him up, intrigued by what he may say next.

"The pain penetrates my heart, but never my soul. Love is a shadow cast, hidden in the darkness. A sad song plays on the radio and I long for the warmth that escapes my empty arms," Jacob rattles off the poetic words, pausing, his eyes and mind giving way to Claire's creative wisdom.

"Rain falls down from the sky, slow at first; then harder," Claire rises to her feet, joining Jacob in the spontaneous delivery of a freshly picked narrative.

Jacob smiles, stirred by Claire joining his poetic party.

Claire continues, "I watch from my windowsill as the droplets dance before my eyes. My heart opens, waiting to be filled like an incomplete puzzle agonizing over its final missing piece." Claire relinquishes the controls back over to Jacob, the two circling around the grass, not performing to each other, but speaking to all of God's creatures.

"The love I have to give is my weakness; it is my pain. I am an Adam without an Eve, and my princess lies down the path less traveled. This is my great drama."

Jacob and Claire look at one another and burst into laughter, satisfied by their grand lyrical accomplishment.

The sky explodes with a deep, earthshaking rattling of thunder. A stern message has been sent.

Jacob and Claire stop giggling, both looking up at the darkening sky which looks ready to burst. The thick dark clouds are sagging low to the ground, their bellies full and barely able to contain the liquid inside. Darkness has fallen upon Starktown.

Nineteen

Ryan bursts through the front door of his vacant home, out of breath, demanding answers.

"Jacob! Claire!" Ryan's calls are met with silence. He rushes from room to room, eventually heading into the kitchen. He's stunned by the mess. Pieces of paper are all over the place, on the walls, the ceiling, the kitchen table.

The counters and floor are covered in flour. Ryan is in absolute shock and confusion.

"What is going on here?" Ryan asks the question out loud, unable to silently deduce any of this.

Ding! Ryan whips his head around to the oven. The digital timer is flashing all zeros. He opens the oven and stares down at a perfectly baked cake. The aroma is tantalizing, suggestively attacking all of Ryan's senses. But the anger inside overwhelms the scent of the freshly baked cake. Ryan grabs two oven mitts from the counter and grabs the tin pan, quickly setting it on top of the stove and closing the warm oven door. Frustrated, Ryan tosses the mitts down on the counter and turns the oven off. Ryan looks around the kitchen wondering what to do next.

The front door is slammed shut.

Ryan jumps away from the counter like he's been shot out of a cannon and rushes towards the front door. Ryan stops abruptly, almost running into the casually strutting Jacob.

"What…Where…How?" Ryan is so angry the words and questions can't find their way out of his mouth.

"Then when and why," mocks Jacob.

"Jacob, I'd like you to start by telling me where Claire is," Ryan says, making the first of his many demands.

Claire enters the house, closing the front door behind her. She smiles, happily waving to Ryan.

"Do I still need you to tell you where she is?" Jacob asks his now fuming older brother sarcastically.

Ryan takes a deep breath, trying to control his anger and keep Claire from any of their family laundry.

"No, but you can tell me where you've been. I tried calling about, oh, well, a few *thousand* times!" Ryan directs the entire brunt of his question at Jacob.

"We were just out driving." Jacob doesn't flinch from answering his big angry brother, showing little respect for Ryan's fury.

"We?" Ryan asks, knowing Jacob has never driven a car before.

"That's right," Jacob asserts proudly, holding his head up high in accomplishment.

"So I'm to assume that you drove as well?"

"Sure. After Claire taught me of course. You know, I didn't know how to drive as of this morning. Now, nearing sunset, I know." Jacob smiles again, victorious.

"You taught him how to drive?" Ryan turns to Claire, still maintaining his poise.

"Yeah. He's not bad. Quick learner," Claire states matter-of-factly.

Ryan turns his attention back to Jacob, who continues to goad his brother, irritating him more and more. Ryan's too smart for Jacob's silent taunts, clasping his internal discontent close to his bones.

"Why don't you go frost the cake," Ryan suggests to his brother.

"Okay. Let's go, Claire." Jacob starts for the kitchen.

"Actually, I need to borrow Claire for a minute." Ryan plays his adult trump card, leaving Jacob in a very shaky position.

"We're partners in this deal. Where she goes, I go," Jacob whines, no longer the suave young man wise beyond his years.

"It's okay, she'll be there in a minute, Jakey." Ryan once again looks down upon his younger brother from a fatherly view.

"I'll be there in a minute," Claire jumps in to settle the tension.

"I'll prep." Jacob saves a little face, including Claire in the process.

"Awesome," Claire says, her response taken from Jacob's dictionary.

Ryan smirks at Claire, recognizing Jacob's influence on her. He waits, watching as Jacob slowly and reluctantly hauls himself out of the living room.

"Awesome, huh?" Ryan says, a little jealous.

"Where have you been?" Claire casts the ball right back into Ryan's court.

"Work! I had to work all day," Ryan explains, as if Claire should have known.

"Oh, we were hoping you were going to get home a little bit earlier. We waited a while."

"Waited for me?" Ryan asks. *This whole day has been one confusing mess.* "Let me ask you something. Did Jacob say I was supposed to be home earlier than…well, right now?" Ryan asks, like a bloodhound, sniffing out a scent of truth.

"It was probably just a misunderstanding," Claire answers, unaware of the true mysteries behind Jacob's true persona.

"Are you aware of what's going on here?" Ryan asks Claire bluntly.

"What do you mean?" Claire naively replies.

"You have to steer clear of Jacob and his world. He lives in his dreams, not in reality. I know it's easy to get caught up in—"

"What are you so afraid of?" Claire interrupts.

"Me? What do I have to be afraid of?" Ryan has admittedly never looked at himself in the mirror.

176

"Of becoming your brother." Claire stares passionately at the man who has captured her heart. He is a small town man with small town ideals, but to her, he is as big as the world has to offer right now.

Ryan looks down to the ground, his reflection almost overwhelming him.

"I love him. I love him like an older brother loves his younger brother. And I love him like a father loves his son."

"I just don't know what to do with him. He doesn't understand rules. He doesn't understand the realities of the world. He hates responsibility and lives by the seat of his pants. He can do that because he doesn't have to put food on the table or pay the bills. He's like that candy you can't get enough of. But too much of that candy can make your stomach get upset. Too much of that candy can make you sick, and in the long run, hurt you."

"Do you know how talented he is? Do you know what he loves to do?"

"Bake?" Ryan has no idea what Claire is talking about.

"His writing. His creativity. You hear it in the words he speaks. He doesn't talk like any other teenager. He has a special essence about him. You know, because that's what also scares you about him."

"He lives in a fantasy world that can't survive here in the real world. He's still a child, Claire. You know how hard it is to be a kid one day and the next have to take over as a parent. Jacob's my responsibility, wholly and completely, not by choice, but by blood," Ryan defends himself passionately, airing everything.

"Jacob's an amazing boy, Ryan. He's so desperate for attention. He'll wear the wackiest clothes and the craziest hats, along with the oddest colors. He's begging, practically crying out for you to notice him. You're both so different, and I haven't earned the right to say any of this, but inside, I know that you both care so much about each other. And regardless of what either of you think, you both need one another. You're family."

"Yeah, we are." Ryan runs his hands through his hair, pacing around the living room. He stares at the pictures of long ago, where Ryan and his baby brother are happy: life in its most innocent and perfect state. He remembers the past, a time when he had so much freedom and so many hopes. Those times are long gone now, as are his hopes and any faint dreams he once held close to his own heart.

"Look Claire, I agree with everything you said. I don't understand Jacob. To an extent, I don't even know who he is. Maybe I don't even know who I am. But there are things about Jacob you don't know. My mother, she and Jacob share something that…" Ryan searches for the words to express the most embarrassing of the Crestwood family secrets.

Jacob comes charging into the room wearing his flour-covered baking outfit. His presence breaks the pensive mood.

"Let's go! The cake is ready!" Jacob proclaims excitedly, as if it were Christmas morning and time to tear open the presents.

"I'm coming, Jacob," Claire says, trying to ease Jacob's enthusiasm in a motherly fashion.

Jacob recognizes Ryan's serious expression and doesn't dare interject in the obviously impassioned discussion. This could be his victory. Claire may finally be his. He dashes back into the kitchen, nearly dancing, as he now becomes even more energized than before.

"He's primed to be let down, Claire. He doesn't know that you view him as this special kid. He thinks you view him as a special man. You can see the glimmer of hope in his eyes. I know that look."

"I'll go talk to him while you get ready. I'll try and explain things to him. It'll be all right. I'm certain he doesn't...but I'll make it clear. That's not at all what this is." Claire understands what she must do.

"Okay. I'm going to get ready. Sorry about all this." Ryan leans in and kisses Claire on the side of the cheek.

Ryan leaves it to her to take care of things. Satisfied, Ryan heads toward the stairs, needing to clean up for his mother's birthday celebration.

Claire takes a step towards the kitchen and stops, a thought striking her as odd.

"Ryan, where is your mother?" Claire poses the question curiously.

"Ask Jacob. Maybe he can enlighten you on *that* subject." Ryan knows full well how much talking Jacob has done with Claire. He leaves Jacob with the toughest of tasks: admitting, with his own words, who he actually is.

Ryan continues up the stairs, leaving Claire to ponder his response.

In the kitchen, Jacob has a plastic can of chocolate frosting opened with two knives sticking out of the thick creamy topping. The yellow cake is warm and well prepared, awaiting its coating of chocolate. Jacob pulls one of the knives out of the container and can't wait to hand it to Claire.

"Thank you," Claire says, graciously accepting the knife.

Jacob grabs a glob of frosting on the knife and begins to frost the warm yellow cake still resting in its tin pan.

"Aren't you supposed to take the cake out of the pan first?"

"It's all relative." Jacob continues to frost the cake side by side with the woman he loves. A Hallmark moment for Jacob and his sweetheart, the two of them hip to hip frosting a freshly baked cake. They could be doing this in the future on the birthday of their youngest child.

"You know what Claire means in Latin?" Jacob asks.

"No…what?" Claire chuckles, amused by the mere asking of the absurd question.

"A rose with many petals." Jacob momentarily turns his body, facing the woman he loves.

"It means all that?" Claire asks, trying to keep things platonic with the love struck boy.

"Maybe." Jacob smiles and turns back to the task at hand, completing the frosting of the smooth and creamy chocolate frosting on the warm yellow cake. It's his mother's favorite.

"What does Jacob mean?" Claire asks, interested in how Jacob views himself.

Jacob again stops frosting and turns, facing Claire, staring deep into her eyes. "An empty heart waiting to be filled." The words flow off Jacob's tongue like butter, the truth never so blinding.

"We need to talk, Jacob." The words ring with a level of seriousness that strikes Jacob as a red flag. His ship is sinking.

"Pez?" Jacob whips out a Superman Pez dispenser, hoping to derail or at least delay the ensuing conversation.

"Uh…" Claire stares at Superman with greater worries on her mind. She doesn't know what to say to a boy that has obviously become desperate. Jacob's no longer suave and in control but now very much so on the defensive, searching his thoughts for a way out; any way out of what may be said over the next few minutes.

"Come on, it's Superman," the words nervously charge out of the young boy's mouth, his heart starting to race.

"I can see that." Claire stares at the superhero, knowing exactly who he is.

"It's the man of steel. How can you refuse someone who can leap tall buildings in a single bound?" Jacob continues, stalling the inevitable.

"I guess I can't." Claire accepts Jacob's peace offering. Two small cherry red pieces of Pez are dropped into her palm. She places them into her mouth, she herself wanting to delay the uncomfortable moment further.

Jacob shoves the dispenser back into his pocket and continues to frost the cake, now nearly completing the job he started with his angel hours before.

"Jacob, I think we need to discuss something." Each word pierces Jacob's skin, penetrating all of the walls and shields he once held strong. Now, his heart is exposed and vulnerable for that fatal shot.

"What?" Jacob dare not make eye contact with her. Somewhere deep inside, the boy is hoping, clinging to his prayers that the worst is not going to be true, that he's lost the war.

"This situation. We need to talk about our situation," Claire dances around the words, walking ever so carefully about a minefield of concerns.

"Frosting a cake?" The highly intelligent boy plays dumb, forcing Claire to spell it out.

"No, Jake. The strange idea of you and me together." It pains Claire to be so blunt, but she manages to get the words out.

Jacob's worst fears have been realized. *I've lost her.* The words ring true as day inside his head. "What's so strange about that?" The boy is relentless, making one last stand on his own behalf.

"I'm dating your brother. And I know it may surprise you, but I kinda like him."

"I thought you liked me." Now Jacob is the boy begging for sympathy.

"I do. And as much as you may be upset, you know that I care about your brother, just as you know that I like you.

But…" Claire's silence alludes to a future far different from the one Jacob grasped close to his heart.

"So I guess this throws a wrench into our marriage plans," Jacob jabs back sarcastically, finding a glimpse of humor in his sea of agony.

"You're great, Jake…"

"But?" Jacob intrudes on Claire's thoughts, now growing impatient, aggressively striving to move the conversation along quickly.

"But you're too young…and you're…"

"Strange," a bitter Jacob chimes in once again.

"No. Not strange, Incredible, but not strange." Claire's words do very little to ease the wave of defeat looming all around Jacob at this ultra-sensitive moment.

"Too young," Jacob sourly repeats to himself, the words striking a tender chord. "How old are you?"

"Twenty-four," Claire says her age with something to prove.

"Ryan's twenty-six, basically twenty-seven. That means you guys are almost three years apart in age," Jacob is trying to prove a point foreign to even himself.

"And you're sixteen," Claire chimes in, not helping Jacob out any.

"But I'll be turning eighteen in just a few hundred days," Jacob's hope dwindles with the last breath uttered in this final word of his final stand.

Claire watches as the sparkle and glow drain away from Jacob's gray, vacant eyes. No longer is he staring at her as the love of his life. No longer do his soft gentle eyes flatter her with witty promises and unique sparks of knowledge. A dark sadness has overthrown the light and hope this impassioned boy once typified.

"It's just…I don't know. I want to be your friend. I need your friendship, Jacob. There's so much more in friendship, and that's what I want from you."

The sky rumbles, thunder rolling over the Crestwood home.

"My friendship?" The words lead to a deafening silence between the two passionate souls.

"Please, Jacob. That's what I want. I want your friendship," Claire says, reiterating her position.

"All right," Jacob agrees gloomily.

"Thank you." Claire, more than anything else, is relieved to have finished the conversation. Just after the final words of the conversation are spoken, the cake is completely covered with a thick blanket of darkness. Jacob and Claire set their knives down.

"Are we ready to go?" Ryan enters the kitchen, now all cleaned up. His world has relaxed, with a cold splash of water, some soap, and the comfort of Claire taking care of things with Jacob.

"Oh, I didn't ask. Where exactly are we going?" Claire poses the question to the two Crestwood boys. Neither brother rushes to answer.

"Our mother lives in a home," Ryan confesses.

"I figured that much," Claire says, not understanding the totality of the word old-age home is the first thought that comes to her head.

"No, a home for…people that need to be taken care of," Ryan tries to be as kind and subtle to his mother's condition as possible.

"Mom's crazy! Ya know, like Looney Toons!" Jacob bluntly points out the asininity of their mother's condition.

"Jake!" Ryan objects to his brother's characterization of their mother.

"I'm crazy, too," Jacob says, equally outspoken over his own mindset, throwing caution to the wind. He no longer considers impressing the fair Claire an option. He is a boy and she is a beautiful woman. All hope is gone.

"Jacob!" Ryan barks at the disturbed young man, appalled by his self-deprecating perspective.

"It's okay." Claire steps in, recognizing the young man's fragile state.

"I'll meet you guys there," Jacob says. He feels suffocated by the room. The air has thinned, his breaths shortening. Jacob's world is shrinking by the second. He rushes out of the kitchen, heading straight for the front door. He swings it open and charges out of the house, the cold cross wind pushes the door wide open, the cold sweeping rage penetrating all shields to the home.

Thunder explodes outside the house.

Ryan and Claire are left in Jacob's wake, silent and upset. Neither of them has an answer.

Thunder rolls and roars, followed by a flash of electricity, momentarily lighting up the world.

Jacob, riding through the darkness, is temporarily exposed by the flash of light, his angry feet pedaling with all his might, his angry heart guiding his every movement. The hot humid summer is encroaching upon what is left of the innocent remnants of summer.

The arctic droplets fall from the sky, smacking the softened soil. The sky completely opens up, the rain pouring down upon the small Illinois town.

Thunder rolls as Jacob rides through the puddles and rain, unfazed by the cold angry storm that now dominates his world. His eyes are focused, his teeth clinched, a grimace permanently cemented on his face. The rage builds behind the boy's eyes, his blackened heart now primed for detonation.

Jacob rides and rides, the town a complete blur. In the blink of an eye Jacob reaches the hospital and care facility. He stops before the building, his feet standing in a puddle of collected raindrops. Jacob's hair is sopping wet, water dripping down the sides of his face, his chin, ears, and even his nose. His clothes are drenched with Mother Nature's natural juice. Jacob's warm breath is visible in the cold stormy air. He's breathing heavily, but shows no signs of being tired.

The thunder crashes just above Jacob's head, the puddles on the ground quivering at the prospect of the evil lurking above.

Jacob drops his bike on the ground with little regard for its safety. He takes determined strides towards his mother's home, drawn by forces unknown to him. Jacob can strike with the force of a queen, but has now been designated to the role of a mere pawn.

Jacob is standing in the puddle of water which has drained off his body onto the floor of the elevator and steps out onto the seventh floor. His zombie-like state is broken by a commotion. Arguing, screaming, the words are unrecognizable, but the voice very familiar. As Jacob turns the corner, he stares down the hall at Claire. She is quiet, showing concern for the situation, the freshly baked cake hiding in a white box resting in her hands. Ryan is speaking with Doctor Wells,

"I don't understand," Ryan responds to the doctor, wanting better answers than the ones already given to him.

"Ahhh! Let me out of here!" Doris's agitation echoes throughout the halls of the mental ward.

"Her medicine was mistakenly withheld this afternoon and she's having an episode. She's going to be just fine," Doctor Wells says, illuminating the situation.

"When can we see her?" Ryan asks, hoping they can get in to see Doris on her birthday, whether she realizes it or not.

"It's best if you come back another day," Doctor Wells urges.

Ryan nods, understanding. He takes the cake from Claire and hands it over to Doctor Wells.

"Do me a favor, Doc. Give her this later and wish her happy birthday for us."

"Sure," Doctor Wells gladly accepts the cake, feeling empathetic for the Crestwood clan.

Jacob rushes by Ryan and Doctor Wells, barely squeezing by.

"Jacob, wait!" Doctor Wells shouts, reaching to grab Jacob.

The boy's too quick, rushing over to his mother's closed door. Jacob frantically tries to open the door, but it's jammed.

"Jacob! No!" Ryan yells out, not wanting his brother to see the ugly truth hiding on the other side of the door.

Ryan runs over to Jacob, his face anguished with concern for his younger brother.

Jacob rears back and throws himself at the door, successfully unjamming it and falling into his mother's room. He looks up, spotting the eyes of two frightened, sweaty orderlies staring back at him.

Doris is in bed, three of four straps successfully holding the majority of her body down. She's struggling, screaming, whining, and crying, using all her might to break free from the chains of sanity. Her face is bright red, veins bulging around her forehead and neck. Her eyes are flaring with madness, leaving only the distant remains of a caring mother.

"Mommy! I want my mommy! Unhand me, you derelicts!" Doris cries out in a senseless storm of raving lunacy.

Jacob stares into his mirror -his other self. His mother's anguished face is a firm reminder of what may be in store for him.

Doctor Wells and Ryan each take one of Jacob's arms, helping him back to his feet, ushering him out of the madness.

"Jacob," Doctor Wells says. He wants to make sure his patient is all right.

"Come on, Jake," Ryan says, solemnly consoling his brother, closing the gateway to dementia and their mother.

Jacob steps out into the hallway, a thousand and one thoughts racing through his mind. Doris's echoing screams; her eyes were filled with a world of chaos and insanity. That's the memory which remains engraved in the young boy's mind. She's insane, the words finally ring true in Jacob's head. That's the bridge which firmly connects the two of them together. That's the answer that explains everything. Everyone else was right. The young Crestwood boy, the outcast, the weird kid, is insane. It all makes sense. He has caught the crazy bug.

"Jacob, you all right?" Claire asks, sensing a sea of trouble behind Jacob's clouded gray eyes.

"I'm going to ride home now." Jacob shows little emotion or flair for life. He's lost his edge. He's somewhere else; somewhere far beyond reality.

"Hey, Jake, why don't we talk for a little while," Doctor Wells says, stepping forward performing his conscientious duty. The three presiding adults show extreme concern for this troubled young man.

"No, thanks. I'm fine." Jacob turns, dragging his body down the hallway toward the elevator.

Claire turns to Ryan, begging with her eyes for him to take control and help his brother.

"Come on, Jake, it's raining," Ryan pleads with his little brother.

"I could use a little rain." Jacob doesn't even bother to turn back around and respond. He calmly walks over to the elevators.

"Shouldn't we do something?" Claire asks Doctor Wells, the entire group of them not sure if anything can be done.

"With the exception of sedating Jacob…" Doctor Wells starts, feeling it's his duty to review all the possible options.

"No! That's not the right answer. Not now." Ryan asserts himself in defense of his brother.

"Let him go. Talk to him. Keep him grounded and keep a close eye on him. If he goes too far, you must bring him here for observation. You must, Ryan." Doctor Wells stares seriously into Ryan's eyes, wanting him to understand the full extent of his position.

Ryan nods subtly, turning to watch as Jacob disappears behind the elevator doors. When the elevator doors once again open, Jacob is no longer in the hospital, he's back spinning his great steel weapon above his head, roaring, intimidating the crowd of people around him.

Twenty

Jacob's worlds begin to merge. He stops spinning, feeling everyone's frightened eyes bearing down upon him. They are all judging him, each peasant and town guard seeing a crazy man. Confident he has fooled them all, Jacob whistles.

The crowd is parted by a galloping white beauty. Before anyone knows what hit them, Jacob gallantly leaps onto his horse and rides off, a victorious smile on his face. He gives a wink to the fair maiden, Claire. She gasps, her heart stealing another moment from the great warrior. Jacob spins his sword around in his right hand, his left grasping tightly onto the reigns.

"The boy is different! He's a heretic!" The shouts of a dismayed, confused old peasant woman. She fingers Jacob as evil, for she has little understanding of the young man's ways.

"He must be destroyed!" Another man shouts.

Soon, the mob has turned again. They want blood, and it's Jacob's neck they want hanged. Once a hero, the people now fear him. The mob, rarely frightened, feels more at ease with tyranny than with that of which they cannot grasp.

Jacob rides his bike through the rain, passing over Broward Bridge, racing through the muddy dirt road. He rises up off the saddle, hoping to gain more speed. Jacob glances back, checking to see if the mob is still following him. He is safely gaining ground away from the angry villagers. Upon turning back, his eyes flare open, yanking back firmly on his white beauty. Jacob is forced to veer off and ride back in the direction of town. His expression changes, no longer the gallant confident hero, but now realizing the turbulent atmosphere surrounding him.

Jacob passes through a couple of narrow alleys, riding unscathed by all the encompassing danger. Jacob jumps off the beauty, smacking her on the behind, sending her off to safety. The horse gallops away, leaving Jacob alone and on foot from here on out. He slithers through the back door of the tavern. The tavern is a safe haven for criminals. The town's guards rarely enter the tavern unless a capital offense hath been committed. A group of soldiers ride by the alley, now vacant of Jacob and his horse, oblivious to the hero's whereabouts.

Jacob's bike is left on the front porch by the opened front door. A trail of muddy footsteps marred by puddles of water lead into the Crestwood home. The rain continues to pound the world around, leaving no doubt to its furious intentions.

Poppers Coffee Shop is open twenty-four hours a day. Teenagers seeking refuge from late night hangovers and souls drowning their sorrows away from the local pubs dominate the midnight crowds at Poppers.

Ryan and Claire are two of the few patrons seated in Poppers on this late night. They each have coffee, mildly warm at best, cooling before them in chipped, faded mugs.

"There's so much you don't know about him," Claire declares to Ryan.

"I raised the boy, Claire! I know him. It's just there are certain parts of him…" Ryan defends himself and his curious relationship with his younger brother.

"And that's the reason! You spent so much time raising him, you forgot to listen. He's got something, Ryan. And I think you might be a little scared to find out what's inside him," Claire charges back at Ryan, trying with everything she has to save the brothers' relationship.

"You don't understand, Claire. It's me or the hospital. You haven't seen him at his worst. I'm willing to do whatever it takes to keep him out of that place. I want him as far away from our mother as possible. I don't know what the answers are. I've prayed for them to come to me, but they haven't arrived." Ryan's eyes tense up, nearly welling with water.

"What could a sixteen year old boy like Jacob have inside that could make him so scary?" Claire asks, with a whirl of confusion surrounding her own judgments and thoughts.

"That's what we're all trying to find out. Claire, as much as much as you know about Jacob, there's so much you don't know. Our mother went into the hospital a few years after my father died. I had just turned sixteen. I thought we were lucky. Jacob could have been placed in foster care, but instead, I took care of him." Ryan reluctantly reminisces about the past.

"And you instantly became his father," Claire empathizes. She for the first time is getting a sense, an understanding of what life is like with Jacob. Not the fairy tale of analogies and free-will, but the harsh realities surrounding the troubled young boy.

"Jacob acts strange sometimes and doesn't do any work, won't go to school. I take the blame for that. But as a young boy, he was there when our father died. He's got a crazy mother and he saw the final breaths of his father. And a doctor tells me he might have the crazy bug that he and my mother may have more in common than we know. And that doctors need to pick his brain to find out what's wrong. I guess that's why I give him so much room. That's the reason I am the way I am with him. As much as I don't know about him, I'm scared to death of losing him."

"But you ignore him sometimes. You pretend you don't hear the strange things he says or see the crazy outfits he wears. So he tries harder and harder, always wanting to test you; to see when you'll break. He's a gift, Ryan. I can see that. He's special." Claire is right and Ryan knows it. The two stop chatting, the stale air of the coffee house proving too much for them. They pay the bill, leave a tip, and exit Poppers.

Ryan zooms through the teaming rain in Claire's BMW, heading back to the Crestwood home.

Jacob slowly and carefully moves about the tavern, attempting to remain inconspicuous. The tavern is crowded as usual, the familiar faces of thugs and scoundrels filling the bar. The tavern reeks of old stale beer and the horrific body odors of the many dirty unkempt thieves.

"Hey! There's that kid again!" Drake jumps up from his seat, his mug of beer crashing down to the ground. Seated beside Drake as usual is Ray, and next to him is Buzz, a thug with far fewer brains than even Ray. The two other men join Drake, rising to their feet. The three thugs then whip out their swords, intimating their desire to fight. They rush around Jacob, surrounding him.

The other patrons in the tavern scatter to the sides, making adequate space for fighting. Nobody rushes out of the tavern, all the evil-minded patrons used to this daily entertainment.

Not giving Jacob time to speak or move, the three men attack, each jabbing forward with their swords.

Jacob works fast to defend himself. A nearby chair provides protection from Ray and Buzz while he smacks at Drake's sword with steel of his own.

Jacob hurls one of his small figurines against the wall, shattering on contact. A small pile of the destroyed, handcrafted pieces are strewn about a corner of his room. Jacob swings his bat around, destroying everything in sight. Jacob's eyes remain open, but the view is far different from anything he has seen before. His vacant gray pupils are fiercely fixed on whatever object Jacob swings at. His mind and soul are working independent of one another, leaving no captain to steer the ship.

The chair is chipped away, bit by bit, by the two thugs who are far stronger and bigger than the suave and valiant young hero. Drake takes a swing at Jacob's head. He ducks below the wild swing and spins around, smacking Drake across the face with the remains of one of the chair's legs. Drake is knocked flat on his back, his sword dislodged from his hand.

Jacob leaps up onto the table, whirling his sword around with a cocksure smile gleaming on his face.

"Come on! I have *faith* on my side!" shouts Jacob, urging the thugs on.

An angered Ray and Buzz each swing wildly at Jacob, one from the left, the other from the right. Jacob leaps up, grabbing on to an old hanging chandelier. The two scoundrels completely whiff on Jacob, striking each other in the face with the butts of their swords.

The onlookers laugh at the show, amused by Jacob's antics. Jacob smiles and gives a nod to the crowd, acknowledging their presence. But a creak and a crack from the heavens quickly bring Jacob back to reality. He looks up, the chandelier losing its grip on the ceiling, not used to the sudden change in weight. The old rusty light fixture gives, crashing down along with Jacob. Smarter than any average man, Jacob leaps off the chandelier just as it breaks free from the roof. The young swordsman lands first on the edge of the table, propelling off just as its thin wooden legs give. Jacob rolls onto the ground, safely away from the chandelier which comes crashing down upon the broken table, old pieces of glass fanning out across the tavern floor.

Buzz and Ray gather themselves, shrugging off their circus like fighting. Ray raises his sword, striking down at Jacob.

Jacob opens his eyes from his dramatic fall to see a sword bearing down upon his neck. He rolls over, narrowly escaping the sharp blade as it smacks the wood floor, drawing a few sparks. The patrons moan and groan with anticipation, rooting for more fighting, more drama.

Jacob spins around and around, gaining momentum. He releases the bat out of his hands as if he were slinging a ball and chain for distance. The bat explodes out of the bedroom window, sprinkling the glass down amongst the pouring rain. A cold burst of wet air streams into the bedroom, accompanied by a frigid cross wind. Jacob's breaths are quick and angry, but the broken glass has caused him to pause, to stall his frantic ways. He senses something and listens for an answer.

"Jacob?" A distant call from downstairs, the familiar voice of his arch-enemy.

Ryan and Claire remain frozen, sopping wet, at the doorway to the home. The front door was completely opened when they arrived. They each look around the house suspiciously, searching for a confused, lost boy.

"Jacob?" Ryan calls out again, waiting for a response of any kind. Maybe a witty comment will come surging down the stairway accompanied by a flamboyant outfit of some kind.

"Jacob!" Now Claire voices her concern, the newly paired couple anxious and distressed, begging for a familiar voice to be at the end of their calls.

Jacob remains cemented to the ground in his bedroom, ignoring the calls from downstairs. His breath is quickened, not from the rage he so successfully displayed moments before, but from the rush of cold wet air clinging to his soft warm skin.

Claire and Ryan jump at the knock on the door, both equally tense and caught off guard by the presence of a stranger.

"Oh, goodness!" Claire holds her chest, staring at an equally soaked Nana. Dressed in a rain coat and carrying an umbrella, the elderly woman hadn't left her home in nearly a year. Now she ventured all the way over to the Crestwood home in the rain, a severe look of panic struck on her face.

"Thank God you're home, Ryan," Nana begins, holding a large burden on her chest.

"You okay, Nana?" Ryan asks this obviously hysterical woman who he knows to be of the mental capacity of his own mother at times.

"Is Billy here?! Please tell me Billy's here! Please!" Nana begs, tears not visible on her rain soaked face, but her red eyes show her to be a deeply disturbed and upset woman.

"I don't think so." Ryan is perplexed by the strangely timed question.

"He went to go fishing with Jacob and he's not back yet. That was so long ago, Ryan. You must help me! You must help me find my Billy boy!" Nana tugs on Ryan's jacket, pleading with all her heart for help.

"Fishing?" Ryan turns to Claire for some help.

"I was with Jacob almost all day. Billy wasn't here." Claire tries to clear the air a little for everyone.

"Oh, my goodness!" Nana yelps, lunging forward onto Ryan, her arms embracing him. Standing in the hallway just out of sight is Jacob. Catatonic still, Jacob understands every word which had been muttered downstairs.

Ryan pats Nana on the back, attempting to console her the best he can. "Nana, let's see what Jacob has to say. I think he may be upstairs." Ryan looks to Claire, checking

195

her to see if they're on the same page. Claire nods, silently agreeing with his mindset.

Jacob flips his sword up into the air, catching the blade end carefully between his fingers. He swings it around, knocking Buzz across the face and out cold. He dances back, flipping his sword back into a ready fighting position.

"Come get some," Jacob urges Ray, his eyes glowing with confidence.

"You're done, little man!" Ray yells angrily, a distinct tone of nervousness overshadowing any confidence he may possess.

Toe to toe, Ray and Jacob strike steel. Jacob plays with the dirty larger thief, not giving in to his strength, but holding back his skill. Jacob smiles and winks at the foul soul, mocking his manhood.

Ray becomes enraged, wildly swinging his sword, losing all concentration.

The eyes of those watching widen, sensing a speedy end to the contest.

Jacob ducks, deflects, and avoids all that Ray has to offer. Sweat is rushing down the sides of Ray's face, his patience and energy growing ever so thin.

And before the giant thief knows what hit him, Jacob, with just a flick of the wrist, knocks Ray's sword up into the air. A stunned scoundrel is left standing before the talented young hero. Like a scene from a classic film, Jacob snatches Ray's sword in his free hand and then crosses both swords around his neck. The thug, virtually helpless, reaches with his free hand down to his boot and pulls out a dagger. Jacob is well ahead of the feeble minded thug, and knees the man in the groin, sending him to the ground.

Ray rolls on the ground in obvious pain and agony.

The audience of drunks and thieves are amused, laughing hysterically while downing another glass of their fine yellow wine.

"Sorry." Jacob smiles and shrugs as he leaves Ray his sword and jumps over his motionless body.

Silent footsteps creep into Ryan's bedroom. His car keys rests safely on his nightstand. Jacob's bloodied hand snatches the keys, not a word spoken, not an expression made.

Ryan flips the switch on in Jacob's bedroom, but no light responds. Ryan pushes the door completely open, struck head on by the cold wet blustery wind racing into Jacob's bedroom through the broken window. The three of them stare at the destruction in shock, no words to describe the scene before them.

"My God," Nana mutters is disbelief, a wave of sadness overcoming her, causing her knees to nearly buckle.

Claire aids the older woman, providing support for her shocked body.

"What happened here, Ryan?" Claire poses a question she doesn't want an answer for.

"Jacob's having an episode. Everything that's happened must have been too much for him. I knew it." Ryan blames himself, angry he didn't stop Jacob, or say something of greater importance to the boy.

The distant starting of an old rusty engine is barely heard over the raging storm outside.

"Wait!" Ryan listens closely, the sound familiar to his ears.

Claire and Nana wait and listen, their pairs of ears unable to pick up whatever sound Ryan's cued in on.

"You hear that?" Ryan asks the two ladies, suspicious of the distant sounding engine.

"What?" Nana has no clue about the foreign sound, a noise she's not accustomed to hearing.

"Sounded like a car starting." Claire searches her hearing the best she can.

"Sounded like my car!" Ryan, now sure of himself, sprints down the hall into his bedroom. He flips on the light and stares at his nightstand, his keys are gone

"My truck! He's got my truck!" Ryan nervously shouts out.

◆

Jacob races toward the creaked open back door. There's no one to stop him on his way out of the dirty thief riddled tavern. The sunlight shining through the door lands directly on Jacob's face. The light, so warm, so inviting, more and more spreads throughout Jacob's body. A feeling of happiness and freedom envelops Jacob's being. He is just strides away from the light, from the angels calling him.

◆

"Nana, call Sheriff Bartlet and stay here! Tell him what's gone on. Tell him we might need some help out there. Claire and I will head out to the lake!" Ryan barks out orders like a drill sergeant, assuming the fatherly role left to him.

"Yes. Please be careful and find them!" Nana's words fade in the ears of a focused Ryan and Claire. They are nearly two full steps out of the house by the time Nana responds to them. Ryan jumps into the driver's seat of Claire's BMW and she follows into the passenger seat. They speed off, the car swerving on the wet muddy terrain, quickly racing down the road.

Jacob's having no better luck with the pickup truck. The rain is pounding the windshield of the trusty vehicle, but the boy barely knows how to work the car. The wipers are working on slow, the speed Jacob has set them to. The rain is shielding the vision of Jacob's two good eyes faster than the rubber blades can sweep the glass clean.

Like and old lady driving an old car, Jacob is leaning forward over the steering wheel, attempting to get the best view possible. His eyes are squinting, the giant sea of water blurring his vision. Jacob's on Thompson Road, that much he's sure of. But the mostly dirt road is unkind on this night, the water leaking through divots in the mud soaked ground, making traction extremely difficult, even for Ryan's sixteen and a half inch Goodyear tires.

The pickup slows to a stop, skidding in a funny side-to-side manner as the tires do their best to grab onto the muddy ground. Jacob hops out of the running car, his feet sinking in the mud the second he hits the ground. The mud, the rain, the cold, they all don't faze Jacob a bit. He runs over to the side of the road, feeling that he's close to Lake Maya. He covers his face from the rain, as if that will give him a clearer view of the world.

"Billy!" Jacob desperately calls out. "Billy! Come on, I'm sorry!" Jacob yells, now with even more urgency in his voice, begging for his friend to magically appear before his eyes. He takes a step further out, momentarily losing his footing and almost falling. Jacob maintains his balance and waits a second longer for a response.

"Jaaaacoooobbbb," he hears in the wind. It's distant but it's there. The cry of a friend far away beckons Jacob further on his journey.

"Oh, God." Jacob nervously mutters. "I hear you, Billy! I'm coming!" Jacob heroically shouts amidst the terrible storm.

Jacob rushes back over to the truck. He shifts the old pickup into drive and sharply turns the wheel to the right. The tires spin on the mud, slowly edging forward in Jacob's desired direction. Although the footing is horrible, Jacob is determined to drive off road, and the wheels catch just enough to do it. The truck bounces up and down, hitting ditches in the mud and overly soaked fresh grass. Jacob turns into the world he loves, the world he so appreciates. But on this night, that world no longer exists; it is a distant memory.

Twenty One

Miles away from the raging storm, Billy, lying on the ground with a trickle of dried up blood next to a cut on his forehead, comes to. His eyes flicker open, trying to grasp his whereabouts.

With a moan and groan, Billy slowly lifts up his pounding head. His head feels like a hundred pounds on a fragile swivel. He struggles to maintain a reasonable level of vision, his eyes discouraged by the light source in the basement. He looks around, noticing the blood on the ground, his dirty porn magazines strewed all about. He thinks, trying to remember how he got here.

"Oh, my head," Billy complains, the pain unlike any headache he's ever felt.

Jacob explodes out of the back door of the tavern, freely walking through the pearly gates into the great warm light.

A sharp pain, a look of shock and fear, and the warmth and happiness flee as quickly as they emerged. Jacob's smile is gone, his freedom ends. He stares into the eyes of the mob, all of which are staring back at the boy, sadly.

"Jacob!" Claire cries out, tears just starting to fall down her cheeks.

Jacob's eyes follow Ryan's sword down to his stomach, the new residence of the aristocrat's steel. The hero is stunned and badly wounded.

Ryan is equally stunned and surprised, almost looking unaware of his own actions. He lets go of the sword, relinquishing any joy or responsibility for his actions. The older brother stumbles backwards, distancing himself from a boy who even he finds intriguing.

Jacob backs up against the wall of the tavern, yanking the sword out of his belly. He grits his teeth, swallowing the inordinate amounts of pain shouting from his stomach. The gallant boy falls to his knees, his time is short.

Bump after bump, Ryan's pickup truck goes chaotically driving over the uneven terrain. The seat belt is all that keep Jacob from flying to the top of the pickup. He's heading down the small hills of the Shawnee, heading straight towards Lake Maya.

The wheels have little control at this point, Jacob's speed increasing as he races down the wet grass, hydroplaning to his desired destination. Jacob hits the windshield wiper control by accident and the speed of the rubber blades pick up. Jacob's face lights up for a moment, now able to get a glimpse of what's on the horizon. He peers through the driving rain, his headlights flashing upon the waters of Lake Maya. Jacob rears back, slamming both his feet on the brakes. But like a hockey puck sliding across the eyes, the truck dives off the edge of the hill, flying into the belly of the cold body of water.

Jacob's face slams against the steering wheel, a blow knocking the boy out. The windshield cracks on contact, as the truck flattens out, momentarily floating in the water. The cold water overtakes the truck and its rear cab collects water, slowly dragging the truck deeper into the lake.

Less than a mile away Ryan is speeding down Thompson Road, the BMW experiencing the same traction problems Jacob had with the truck. Ryan and Claire struggle to see, but all four of their eyes take on the strain, searching with all their might for any sign of Jacob or the truck.

"Are you sure he went this way?" Claire asks Ryan.

"I know Jake. Here's out here somewhere," Ryan proclaims with the utmost confidence, his eyes frantically searching through the terrible weather conditions.

In a road with no lights, only pitch black darkness and a wicked storm, Ryan spots a distant flicker of hope.

"What's that?!" Ryan points towards the faded light source, praying for a miracle.

He slows the car down, the two of them fighting the rain for a better view. Claire recognizes their location. Two familiar oaks by the side of the road jog her memory.

"This is it! This is the place! This is where your brother took me, where the lake is!" Claire declares confidently.

Ryan and Claire exchange a brief breath of worried air. They quickly rush out of the car into the angry storm.

Thunder rolls in the sky above, asserting its well-known presence even more.

Ryan leads the way, fearlessly sliding along mud and grass out to a point overlooking Lake Maya.

The sight is gruesome. The pickup truck is systematically being swallowed by the hungry lake. The truck's lights are barely poking their heads out of the water with every other inch of the vehicle fully submerged.

"Oh, Jesus!" Claire yelps in fear for Jacob's life.

"Jacob! Jakey!" Ryan screams, sprinting down the slippery slope with no care for his own bodily safety. He falls down, sliding down the side of the hill, moving as quickly as he can to the lake's mouth. "Jake!" Without hesitation, Ryan dives into the water, swimming over to the truck.

"I'm coming, Jakey! Hold on! Hold on!" Ryan yells desperately, doing his best to fight the cold, the water, and time.

Claire moves timidly down the hill, the footing absolutely horrendous in the worst storm to hit the small town in years. Claire rushes over to the side of the lake, distressed, as the rain and wind batter her face. She prays, watching as Ryan reaches the location of the truck.

The cabin of the truck is filling with water through cracks in the rear cab and the windshield. Jacob remains motionless in the car, blood streaming down the right side of his face, his eye socket a puddle of crimson despair.

Ryan dives underwater and swims to the truck with urgency. Ryan reaches the truck, looking inside the cab from the driver's side window. He see his unconscious brother, the blood rushing down the side of his face while the water level is quickly rising around him. Neck high, Jacob's limp body slumps over in the water, his face and mouth separated from any source of oxygen.

"Jacob!" Ryan yells, begging his brother to come to. He reaches for the door handle, yanking back with all his might. It is to no avail, the outside pressure of the water makes it impossible for Ryan to open the door. He bangs on the driver's side window, but there's not enough force behind his blows. With the air in his lungs gone, Ryan is forced to retreat above water.

He bursts up out of the water, taking one large gasping breath and dives back down to his brother's rescue. Ryan heads for the windshield, noticing the crack already established by the crash. He tries to kick the windshield open, but does little damage, only cracking it a little more. With nothing to support his body, he has little strength in his legs. Ryan pulls himself close to the window, clasping onto the outside of the car with his left hand. He makes a fist with his right and reaches back. He pulls his entire body forward and strikes the sharp thick glass with his right hand. The glass shards dig into Ryan's skin as he breaks through the small hole. A cloud of blood immediately swarms around the activity. Ryan shoves half his arm through the glass opening, his eyes nearly closing from the excruciating pain. He latches onto the windshield with his right forearm and pulls back, ripping nearly the entire slab of glass off the front of the truck. Ryan's vision is marred by his own blood, now a huge cloud of red smoke infecting the entire crash area. He reaches down, maintaining his focus despite the extraordinary pain, and grabs his little brother.

"Ryan! Jacob!" Claire yells, pacing back and forth, ankle high in the water. Seconds go by, her nerves nearly overwhelming her. Every second seems like eternity. Then, an eruption out of the water.

Ryan bursts up to the surface, gasping for air his lungs desperately need. Clinching his left arm around Jacob, Ryan struggles over toward the lake's edge.

Claire rushes out into the water, going nearly chest deep to aid Ryan with the unconscious Jacob.

Ryan, exhausted, weak, and out of breath orders Claire, "Get him to shore."

Claire drags Jacob the rest of the way while Ryan struggles in the water, his entire right arm covered in his own blood. Deep cuts, many of which are down to the bone, cause Ryan to nearly pass out. He pulls off his long sleeve shirt and ties it around his biceps, trying to limit the amount of blood he's quickly losing.

Claire has started CPR on Jacob and is unaware of Ryan's condition.

Two paramedics followed by Sheriff Bartlet come racing over the side of the hill.

"There!" Sheriff directs the emergency technicians to the lake's edge. The three of them rush down the side of the hill, all recognizing the seriousness of the moment.

"Hurry! Hurry!" Claire sees them coming and urges them to help.

The paramedics move Claire to the side and instantly administer CPR to the boy, relieving Claire.

"Jacob! Come on," Claire urges, exhausted.

"Come on, Jake!" yells Sheriff Bartlet, his words shouted with authoritative demand.

Claire turns to find Ryan. She sees him lying on his back, barely able to keep his eyes open. She crawls over to his side and sees the massive amounts of blood he's losing from the deep cuts in his arms.

"Ryan…oh, God. Those are deep." Claire looks Ryan's arm over in shock.

"Just get Jake to the hospital," Ryan, so very weak, mumbles to Claire.

"You're badly hurt!" Claire says, knowing Ryan needs serious medical attention.

The situation is becoming nearly fatal for both Crestwood boys.

"We've got a heart-beat!" One of the paramedics shouts.

"Let's get him to the ambulance!" The other paramedic shouts, the two of them carrying Jacob's fragile body back up the hill.

"Where's Ryan?" Sheriff Bartlet shouts, only seeing the drenched Claire and not the injured man lying beside her.

"Right here and he's hurt! He's hurt bad, Sheriff!" Claire shouts over the driving wind and rain which just won't give.

"Ryan! Oh, good Lord!" Sheriff Bartlet recognizes the elder Crestwood's injuries.

"Ryan? Ryan?" Claire desperately calls for Ryan's attention, but his eyes are closed, and his lights are out.

"Get one side! We gotta get him out of here!" The sheriff assesses Ryan's situation as critical and the two usher his body up the side of the hill, following behind Jacob and the paramedics.

Once loaded into the ambulance, the two Crestwoods are rushed to the emergency room, neither speaking a word, nor opening an eye.

Their ultimate fates are yet to be decided.

Twenty Two

Claire is passed out in a visitor chair, exhausted from her long night. She's dressed in a nursing outfit, her body and hair mostly clean from the long night before.

"Ma'am? Ma'am?" The nurse speaks softly, attempting to garner Claire's attention.

"I'm up. I'm up!" Claire rises groggily, ready to hear any news about the boys.

"You can see him now," the nurse says, giving Claire the green light to visit the recovery room.

"Thanks." Claire picks her tired body up and quickly wakes up, rubbing her eyes open.

Lying in a bed with his arm in a cast is Ryan. He momentarily grins at the sight of Claire. His hair is a mess and his eyes are darkened from exhaustion, but this once stale, narrow minded man has a new glow in his sea blue eyes.

"Come in," Ryan graciously invites Claire into his room.

"You finally woke up." Claire smiles as if grateful everything has worked itself out.

"Yeah." Ryan smiles with a relaxed comfort.

"How's Jake doing?" Ryan asks, as if already knowing good news is on the way.

"He's sleeping and looking okay. They're running some more tests right now. That little brother of yours has a head nearly as hard as yours," Claire jokes, bringing relieved smiles from the two of them.

"He takes after his brother," Ryan makes fun of himself, again drawing a brief chuckle from the two of them.

"I'm sorry, Ryan," Claire apologizes out of the blue, stepping closer to Ryan's bedside.

"About what?" Ryan asks curiously, having no idea what Claire could be apologetic about.

"At dinner...and before. Just all the stuff I said. I was out of line to judge you or your brother when I can't even deal with things myself. I'm sorry."

"Don't be. You were right, Claire. You were right about a lot of things. Thank you for being so honest." Claire and Ryan clasp hands, thankful everything is going to be all right.

"I was really scared last night. I find a guy I like and he goes diving into a lake with no respect for his own body, trying to be some kind of hero," Claire jokes with Ryan. "I don't know, sounds like trouble to me." A devilish smile follows Claire jesting.

"I try to be a renaissance man. I don't like holding myself back from anything." Ryan continues the game, Claire trying to hold in her laughter, nodding along with the response. The two share a silent moment, staring into one another's eyes.

"Hey, it's okay now. It's all over," Ryan comforts Claire.

Claire smiles, running her hands through Ryan's hair, attempting to fix the mop on top of his head. Her eyes catch Ryan's, their lips already so close to each other. She leans down, bringing her lips to Ryan's mouth. A gentle, tender kiss.

"I'm going to go check on Jake and see if he's awake yet," Claire says, blushing a bit and breaking the romantic moment.

"Wait, I wanna come too. Get the nurse in here."

"Stay there. You're not going anywhere, mister. The nurse told me you can't be movin' around just yet so keep your butt right where it is!" Claire lays down the law to her man.

"Please?" Ryan begs, wanting so badly to get a look at his little brother.

"I'm such a sap." Claire helps Ryan to his feet and they exit the room together.

Jacob's head is wrapped with white head dressing while his left hand is set in a cast. He's hooked up to numerous machines monitoring his vitals. Jacob's staring out at the window, a bright sun striking his face. He looks directly into the bright light, his eyes fighting through the overwhelming glare. He searches his thoughts for answers; answers to how he got here, and why.

Claire and Ryan quietly step into Jacob's recovery room. Ryan's left arm is fixed around Claire's neck, for support, and for simple closeness.

"Is Billy okay?" a sedated Jacob asks, barely turning his head to acknowledge Ryan and Claire's presence.

"It seems you weren't the only one to hit your head yesterday," Claire begins, finding humor in the irony. "Billy hit his head in his basement and knocked himself out cold. He's at home right now."

"I think Nana's boarded up that basement though. You and Billy are gonna have to sneak peeks at those dirty magazines somewhere else," Ryan jokes, the couple in a jovial mood.

"Good." Jacob remains subdued as he turns away from the bright light. "Tell him I'm gonna kill him," Jacob jokes too.

Claire leaves Ryan's side, moving over to the blinds. She twists the string, the light on Jacob's face turning to darkness.

"Let's work on getting you back on roller blades before you go killin' anyone," Ryan continues, joking with his little brother, this time drawing a momentary smirk. "How ya feelin' little brother?" Ryan moves next to Jacob's side, now expressing concern.

"Sore and light-headed." Jacob gently pats the outside of his head dressing, the bandages causing him some discomfort.

"You had me scared, Jake." Ryan cringes as he sets himself down on the bed next to Jacob. He leans over, doing his best to give his little brother a hug using his one good arm. On his way back up, Ryan kisses Jacob on the forehead. "I love you kid. You mean the world to me. And…no more driving for a little while, okay?" Ryan grins, alleviating the emotionally charged moment.

"Okay," now Jacob displays a complete smile.

"That's so wonderful." Claire smiles, almost in tears over the touching moment.

"Girls," Jacob comments, mocking Claire's emotional state. Ryan smiles and nods agreeably, his little brother finally learning something from him.

Ryan lifts himself back off Jacob's bed, again wincing from the pain of his fresh wounds. "Hey, Ryan?" Jacob asks for his brother's attention, a question already in mind.

Ryan turns back to Jacob. "Yeah, Jake?"

"Am I crazy…ya know, like Mom?" Jacob's eyes yearn for an answer to a problem he can't solve.

"No, kid. You're not crazy, not one bit, and don't listen to anyone that tells you such lies. You hear me?" Ryan has never been so sincere in his life, truly believing the words that ramble out from his heart.

Jacob nods and cracks a smile, feeling the full weight of support from his older brother, for the very first time.

"Mr. Crestwood, what did I tell you?" The nurse echoes her dissatisfaction over Ryan's newfound desire to be mobile in a motherly. With her hands on her hips, she scowls at Ryan, waiting for a response.

"I know, I know. Back to my dungeon, Nurse Ratchet," Ryan replies sarcastically. "See you soon, okay?" Ryan says to Jacob in passing as he heads towards the nurse, on his way back to his room.

"Cool," A simple, Jacob-esque response.

"I'll come by in a minute," Claire tells Ryan.

Ryan throws up his hand as if to say goodbye, struggling to walk as the nurse ushers him away.

"You had us scared," Claire says to Jacob stating the obvious.

"You? I flew into a lake. I was terrified! Although, it was kinda awesome, now that I think about it."

Claire shakes her head at Jacob, who can't keep a straight face, busting into laughter. Claire laughs along with the brave young man, shaking her head at his sarcasm over such a serious experience.

Jacob adjusts the lower half of his body, struggling mightily to move. He grits his teeth and uses his free hand to help himself get comfortable.

"Are you all right?" Claire asks with compassion and a dash of concern.

"I'm fine. It's just my legs are a little tingly and numb. I think it's some of this medicine they've been pumping into me." Jacob looks over the many tubes running all around his bed. "Claire…I know this is a lot to ask for, but… can I have one kiss?" A very shy Jacob musters up the courage to have his angel ponder his one wish. The bravery from his accident has obviously carried over. But he's still a boy at heart, his face turning bright red, his mouth becoming dry, while his eyes drop down to his bed sheets, avoiding all contact with Claire's sparkling gems.

Claire smiles, flattered and amused by the young man's request. She doesn't have an opportunity to respond before the nervous boy continues on.

"I figure this is the best time for me to ask, being that I'm so hurt and all." Jacob cracks a smile, playing the bedridden card.

Claire slowly leans in close to Jacob. He feels her coming, but refuses to look up, the sight would be too overwhelming for him to handle.

"Don't you think?" The words stumble out of Jacob's nervous, frozen lips.

"Shut-up Jacob." The beautiful angel swoops in, nearly touching Jacob's nose with her own.

Jacob closes his eyes, clinching them tightly, as if he were facing a firing squad. Every muscle in his body is paralyzed. Then, her soft lips caress the side of the gallant young hero's cheek. A gentle sweet, innocent kiss that sends millions of tingles racing throughout the brave young man's body. Jacob's heart races and he breaks into a satisfied smile as Claire slowly leans back away from his face.

"Cool," is the only word to fall out of Jacob's mouth as his eyes remain closed, savoring the moment forever.

"Now rest and get better. I'll see you in a little bit."

Claire exits the room while Jacob continues to savor his kiss. There is no better cure than a kiss.

Twenty Three

Hours later, nightfall has led to a deep slumber for Ryan and Claire. She sleeps, curled up in a small cot set up next to Ryan's bed. The two are sound asleep when Claire comes to. A strange, odd commotion is being made down the hall. The chattering and rattling of machinery causes her to awaken. With a yawn and a stretch, Claire rises to her feet, now fully aware of all her surroundings. Curious, Claire slowly moves to the doorway and peeks her head out to see what the commotion's all about.

Lying on the ground, stabbed in the stomach, the blood now soaked clean through his ragged clothing, Jacob remains with his eyes shut. The crowd is silent around Jacob's unconscious and motionless body. A deep collective breath has left everyone speechless. No cheering, no applauding over a kill, no stomping for blood, and no smiles.

All watch as a boy lay lifeless on the ground.

Until…a cough rouses everyone's attention. Jacob coughs, his heart fighting to stay alive.

Ryan, Claire, and the mob are in shock over Jacob's resurrection. Frightened and unsure of what to do, Ryan grabs his sword off the ground.

The miraculous young boy uses all his strength and will to sit up, his eyes flickering open like a robot that just got recharged.

"You're alive!" shouts an exuberant Claire, elated to see her hero still of this world.

"It would appear so." Jacob stares angrily at the cowardly aristocrat. He reaches on the ground next to him, clinching his sword with one hand, while he uses the other to press against his deep stomach wound. Jacob uses his sword to help lift his ailing body up off the ground. It takes every last bit of strength in his body, but Jacob manages to stand almost perfectly upright. He raises his sword, pointing it at Ryan's heart. He stares down the shiny blade and with all his heart, with all his bravery, with all his heroism, Jacob scares the life out of the unworthy soul of a man.

"Neither death nor your hate can stop my love. Now drop your weapon or I will be forced to slay you," Jacob threatens the man, as if he were prepared to fight a dragon. And by the look of his eyes, everyone believes it.

Ryan slowly lowers his sword down to the ground, attempting to keep one eyes on Jacob's threatening blade. He sets his steel down on the ground.

"I didn't mean it, Jacob. I'm sorry. I love you, brother. I love you," the words roll off Ryan's tongue sincerely, begging his little brother for forgiveness.

Jacob stares at Ryan, not wanting to hurt him. He feels anguish and then he feels a sharp pain in his stomach that brings him to his knees. Jacob falls back down to the ground, a giant hand reaching into his soul, attempting to drag his being out from his human home.

Claire rushes down the hall of the hospital towards Jacob's recovery room, realizing it's him that the commotion is over. She walks quickly at first, then runs as she is reassured something is happening in Jacob's room.

"No." the breathy word barely slips out of Claire's mouth, not wanting to believe anything is wrong.

The concern is almost too much for her to handle. The tears start rolling down her cheeks, sensing something seriously amiss.

"Somebody call a doctor!" Claire shouts as she bends down to her hero's side. She places her hand on top of his bloody hand, doing everything she can to try and stop the bleeding.

"It's too late for that, my dear." Jacob eases Claire's hand off his bloody stomach and chest as his life drains out all around him.

Claire takes Jacob's bloody hand in her own, clinching it tight. "No, you must fight," Claire orders with tears streaming down her face. She begs the young hero.

"I have fought my last fight. I have showed the world all it needs to see. All that has kept me here is my one last desire; my one last wish," Jacob stares up into Claire's sad longing eyes.

"What would that be my sweet Jacob?" Claire runs her free hand along the side of Jacob's face.

"I will not leave this earth until I have one fair kiss from my one true love."

"Then I shall never kiss you and you will live forever." Claire cracks a smile amongst her sea of pain.

Jacob lets out a chuckle, amused by Claire's logic, but he's rudely interrupted by pain in his head. "I think the gods have other plans," Jacob points out. Jacob passes out, his body gone limp.

"Jacob!!!" Claire screams at the top of her lungs.

Nurses sprint by Claire into the room and she is immediately shoved out of the way. A doctor races inside.

Claire backs away slowly to the doorway, a nurse attempting to usher her out of the room. But the nurse's words are unheard in Claire's stake of shock. She stares at the boy, a look of horror overcoming her face, tears welling in her eyes. Just moments before, she was in his recovery room and he was laughing and joking. Now, his monitor has flat lined and doctors are frantically attempting to resuscitate this shining soul whose light is diming by the second.

"Oh, God," Claire whispers under her breath as she is pushed out of the room, her mouth hanging open in shock.

"Please, my precious and beautiful Claire, give me my one wish, my final request," Jacob begs of his true love.

"All right. If that's all you need to make you happy and take you on to that better place, then you shall have it with all my heart." Claire slowly leans in and kisses Jacob softly on the lips. Their eyes are both closed, each of them savoring every last drop of this moment, the loving pouring out of them. She leans back and sees a smile struck on Jacob's face. The sight of Jacob's grin brings relief to Claire. But his eyes remains closed and his smiles fade away.

"Jacob!" Claire screams, crying, hoping for one of the many miracles Jacob has left in his pockets.

The doctors defibrillate Jacob over and over again, but to no avail. The angels have gathered around the shining spirit.

Claire's tears fall over Jacob's lifeless body as the mob stares in shock. They've lost more than they'll ever know. Who was this boy that at times amused them with his antics that amused him with his chivalry that inspired them with his hope? Now, they will never truly know. Their shouts and accusations haunt each and every one of them. Just now, for the first time, they realize the folly of their ways.

Claire rests her head atop of Jacob's still chest. She holds him for the last time, closing her eyes, cherishing the moment.

Claire watches in disbelief, her mouth hanging open, the tears pouring down her face. She is helpless as she watches the young boy cling to the last moments of his life.

Moments go by. They seem like hours as Claire drags herself back into Ryan's recovery room. He remains fast asleep, unaware of any of the late night occurrences. It's morning now. A new day is dawning. Claire's face tells the story of a tragedy. Her eyes are red, bloodshot, with dark rings from crying. Her cheeks are puffy, her nose is sniffling.

Ryan's eyes open upon hearing Claire enter the room. He yawns, just coming to. It's every other morning for Ryan. "Didn't sleep so good, huh?" Ryan points out, remembering that he recommended that Claire go home to sleep. But as he stares at her sadness, he knows a lack of sleep didn't cause the look in her eyes, or the expression on her face.

"Claire, what's the matter?" Ryan sits upright, becoming alarmingly concerned. Now he senses something is very wrong and fears the worst.

Claire drops her head and cries, not having the heart to look Ryan in the eye in this, the most dramatic and emotional of all moments. "It's Jacob." The words barely escape from Claire's reluctant lips, overshadowed by her explosion of emotions.

Ryan's mouth drops open, his face agonizing with the thought. His eyes water, begging for there to be a light at the end of this very dark tunnel.

"They said he had a blood clot in his brain. They tried to help, but there was nothing they could do. They couldn't help him, Ryan. He's gone." Claire emotionally breaks down, sitting on the bed next to a stunned Ryan. Claire hides her face in her hands, crying hysterically.

"Oh, Jakey." Ryan looks around his recovery room, tears racing down his face. His eyes don't know where to go, flashing back and forth across the room, confusion and hysteria overcoming the last remaining male Crestwood. "Oh, Jake, I'm so sorry," Ryan cries. Claire turns and embraces Ryan, the two of them grieving together, in each other's arms.

"He never hurt anyone, Claire. He was so innocent. He just wanted to be happy. That's all. Oh, Jakey!" The surge of emotion from Ryan leaves him speechless, hiding his tears on Claire's shoulder and her tears on his. They embrace, their sobbing continuing for hours.

———◆———

A day later, with his arm in a cast, Ryan had the unenviable task of reporting to Doris Crestwood the events that took place just two nights before. He moves slowly down the dark hallway, Ryan's face bland, stoned with the sadness that has consumed him over the last forty-eight hours. He enters Doris's room and simply begins, "Hi, Ma. I've got some bad news."

A few seconds of near silence go by as Ryan explains what has happened. A pause and then an ear piercing wailing of sadness fills the air of the entire building.

Doris's cries echo through the quiet halls of the ward. "No! Not my Jacob! Not my Jakey!" Doris screams over and over again, her tears flowing just as Ryan and Claire's had just a night before. "Oh, Ryan, why Jakey? Why'd they have to take Jakey?" Doris cries and cries, Ryan yielding his shoulder to her as a cushion. The only tears left in Ryan's tired, emotionally drained body slowly trickle down his cheek as his mother wails on and on, mumbling words of sadness, begging for answers she will never get in this lifetime.

Twenty Four

Jacob's room remains just as he left it three nights before, mutilated by a fit of insanity. Ryan reaches up to the light fixture and screws in a bulb, injecting a bit of light in the room of absolute darkness. Ryan surveys the destruction, his eyes moving about all the brutal chaos. Broken glass, broken wood, clothes torn and thrown about, artifacts left decapitated and smashed beyond recognition, this is what remains of the boys dwelling. A cool breeze sweeps through the lifeless room, the cold crisp clean air that follows a good storm. Ryan spots Jacob's treasure chest, the only item in the room untouched, left in pristine condition despite the storm that raged through everything else. He moves over to Jacob's prized possessions. He lifts open the chest revealing the hundreds of poems, stories, and thoughts Jacob had accumulated over his short life. He looks through a piece of paper with a short poem on it. He reaches down and picks up a short story covering the front and most of the back of the page. He grabs another, then another, looking through page after page, faster and faster. Ryan fixes his eyes and his head quickly rises up, as if a lightning bolt struck him. He has a purpose, something he now knows that he never knew before. He rises to his feet, releasing the inspirational work back down into its home. He moves over to the window, his face feeling an extra charge of cold. He closes his eyes, accepting the frigid air as if it were his own.

Yes, this is it. This is the feeling he sought. This is what he needs to do.

Ryan heads downstairs and moves quickly to Claire's BMW, the only car parked in his driveway. He takes step after step, gliding across the ground as if walking on air. He has a purpose, he knows what he must do.

Ryan steers the car down Thompson Road, the trip seemingly taking only a moment in time. Upon arrival he slowly moves out of the car, stepping across the soft healthy grass of the Shawnee. He moves to Jacob's favorite spot, as if drawn there by a force unbeknownst to himself.

Ryan stares out at the glorious sky, millions of stars shining extra bright in the clear cold night's sky. He shivers for a moment, but those feelings of winter soon pass. He looks over at beautiful Lake Maya. Her waters sparkle, glistening with fresh rain water, replenishing her deep thirst. The world is so peaceful, so fresh. Ryan sees all this for the first time. It's so glorious.

Ryan moves down the grassy knoll, heading to the shores of Lake Maya. The fresh memories of the accident and desperate attempt to save Jacob's life are but a distant memory at this moment. Now is not the time for mourning, it is the time for enlightenment. Ryan begins removing his clothing, slowly at first, then quicker and quicker. His shoes, socks, jacket, shirt, and pants all fall to the soft dirt at his feet. Dressed only in his boxers, Ryan steps toward the lake in a euphoric trance.

His toes touch the edge of the frigid waters, his breath very visible in the icy fresh air. He stares out at the friendly body of water, a sweet voice calling him closer and closer. He steps forward, the water approaching his ankles in height. The cold battles Ryan's plans, but he will not be denied. He continues on, the water now waist high.

"God, it's so cold, Jakey. The water's so cold." Ryan momentarily dips his head back, as if speaking with his younger brother. Satisfied he has moved the correct distance out, Ryan slowly turns, facing the shore. He extends his arms out, the chattering of his teeth ignored by all his clear and concise thoughts. His eyes are squeezed tightly shut as Ryan lets his inhibitions go. He falls backwards into a whole new world.

His vision is blurred and unclear at first, as his nearly two hundred pound body rests just below the surface of the water. But within seconds, he floats up to the surface, at least enough that only the sides and back of his face is gently bouncing beneath the water's surface.

Quick cold-laced breaths come from Ryan's nose and mouth, while his teeth chatter uncontrollably. For a second, his mind and body are shocked by the familiarly frigid waters of Maya.

Ryan's vision soon becomes clear, making eye contact with the millions of twinkling stars smiling down upon him. A sense of calm and bliss override the feelings of cold. No more chattering of teeth or shortness of breath. No, just the pure essence of the moment. A smile overcomes Ryan's face as he feels exhilarated and inspired by the view.

A single star shoots across the sky leaving a tail that must have been thousands of miles long. Before it can disappear, another joins it. Then another, and another. Soon, hundreds of stars are streaking across the sky. Ryan holds his breath, the show amazing him. He can hardly believe his eyes. The beautiful scenery has taken him to a place he never knew existed.

"Jacob! Oh, God, Jacob! I can see it! I can see all of it! Ha! I can see it!" Ryan shouts in excitement as he watches star after star dance before his eyes, streaking all around the great spirited canvas.

Ryan laughs as the stars, thousands at a time, go streaking, some leaving colorful trails of dust in their wake. The sight is breathtaking.

"Ha-ha!" Ryan shouts once again in enjoyment, like a kid in a candy store. "Jacob, I see it! Yes! Yes!" Tears race down the sides of Ryan's face as he experiences the pinnacle of his happiness, finding all the wonders overwhelming. "Oh...yes!"

Twenty Five

Five years later, the Crestwood household still stands tall. A new glow reflects off the refurbished two-story home. There's a new coat of white paint on the windows outlined in forest green, a nice contrast. The walkway is decorated with the beautiful violets that Jacob so loved. The front lawn is now lush green, well-kept and full of life. A freshly painted white picket fence encircles the front lawn while a four-year old Golden Retriever rests comfortably on the front lawn, sleeping happily on his side.

"Jacob, come on down!" Claire calls out from the base of the stairs. Her hair's a bit shorter, but for the most part, an older wiser Claire, still angelic and beautiful, hasn't changed too much in the last five years.

The inside of the house has been overhauled too. Bay windows have been added around the dining room with all the antiques gone, packed away in storage. New couches, light fixtures, rugs, paintings, and chairs bring new life to what used to be a stale old world.

"Come on, we're late," Claire urges.

"Sorry, mommy!" The pitter-patter of Jacob Junior's three-year old feet come hopping down the light blue carpeted stairs.

She smiles upon seeing the sparkling gray eyes of her son. Claire takes her young boy's hand and they head out the front door.

Ryan, a few pounds heavier, his face clean and shaven, rests comfortably in the driver's seat of his new Ford pickup truck. Claire's two-year old Mercedes is dwarfed by the shiny new six passenger custom white truck. A big grin is displayed upon his face once his wife of nearly four years and their special boy come walking out of the house. Jacob Jr. takes the initiative, running over to the car, his small little legs doing their best to stride forward.

The happy family load into the truck.

"Everyone buckle up." The dad patiently waits for everyone to get set. "What took everyone so long?"

"Sorry, Daddy." Jacob Jr. appears apologetic. "Mommy wouldn't get out of the bathroom." Jacob Jr. barely gets the lie out of his mouth before he displays his innocent precious smile.

"Oh, my goodness, lie!" Claire laughs, looking at her son in shock over his betrayal. Claire reaches into the back seat where Jacob Jr. is trapped in his child seat. She sadistically tickles his belly. The boy futilely tries to protect himself, giggling uncontrollably.

Today the family has a couple of important stops to make. First, Jacob Jr. will get to visit his grandmother, who resides in the same home she's lived in for the last nine years; a special room in the Starktown psychiatric building.

"Now, what did I tell you?" Doris asks Jacob Jr., the two of them sitting alone in her room, each holding five playing cards in front of their faces.

"Never hit on fifteen!" Jacob Jr. is excited to throw out an answer that he thinks is correct.

"Oy! This is poker!" Doris smacks her forehead with her free hand.

"Oh, poker! That's when you get forty percent of my winnings," Jacob Jr. now understands the game they're playing.

Doris smiles, proudly patting young Jacob Jr. on the head. "That's my boy," she says, loving his brainwashed response.

Ryan enters the room carrying a hard covered black book. "What are you guys doing?" Ryan looks his mother over suspiciously.

"It's private, right Grandma?" Jacob Jr. turns to Doris.

"It sure is." She gives another proud grin to her grandson.

"Here's a copy," Ryan gives his mother the black book.

She gladly accepts it, her eyes glowing with anticipation. She gently runs her fingers along the gold lettered title: *Jacob's Tales*. She smiles, a whole other level of satisfaction and pride warming her blood. She takes a deep breath, feeling a great swell of emotion emanating from inside her heart.

"Thank you," she says, a breathtaking, sincere gratitude expressed from Doris to her son.

"We gotta meet your mom back at the party now. Kiss Grandma goodbye." Ryan directs his three-year old son.

Jacob Jr. approaches his grandmother and gives her a big hug. They exchange a kiss on the cheek and he backs away toward his father.

"Bye, Grandma." Jacob Jr. waves.

"Bye-bye, sweetie."

Ryan kisses his mother goodbye and the two Crestwood men head out of the room.

Less than two miles away from the hospital, a small housing development has been established. It is the first expansion in Starktown in many, many years. Most of the homes are in development, but one perfect two-story model has been created. The sign reads: Crestwood Estates. Red and white flags blow proudly in the wind, asserting the new look in town.

Families, many of them young, are perusing the area, enjoying the free food and party atmosphere. Kids are running around, having a good time. All of Ryan and Claire's friends, familiar faces a plenty, are there enjoying their great achievement. An older Billy is accompanied by his girlfriend of four years, Cara. They are hand in hand as they make their way through the fun block party.

The new development gives new hope to an otherwise old town. There is new life being injected into the old stale world. Starktown is better off for having known Jacob. For that matter, so is everyone else.

THE END

About the Author

A creative soul all his life, Brett Scott Ermilio began by writing serial stories for his friends, integrating them into different worlds as early as middle school. By high school, Brett was writing full-length movie scripts.

Brett won a screenwriting contest receiving the Best Screenplay Award for his script, Jacob. That story was turned into his first fictionalized novel. Brett also wrote the biography, Going Platinum: KISS, Donna Summer and How Neil Bogart Built Casablanca Records. Going Platinum was released in hardcover in November of 2014 with paperback due out November 2015.

Brett currently resides on the Jersey Shore with his nine colorful roommates: his loving wife, four beautifully chaotic children, three small yapping dogs and one moody fish.

www.ingramcontent.com/pod-product-compliance
Lightning Source LLC
LaVergne TN
LVHW051045080426
835508LV00019B/1721